Globalization and Postmodern Politics

Globalization and Postmodern Politics

From Zapatistas to
High-Tech Robber Barons

Roger Burbach

Pluto Press

LONDON • STERLING, VIRGINIA

ARAWAK
publications

KINGSTON, JAMAICA

First published 2001 by Pluto Press
345 Archway Road, London N6 5AA
and 22883 Quicksilver Drive,
Sterling, VA 20166–2012, USA

www.plutobooks.com

and Arawak publications
17 Kensington Crescent, Kingston 5, Jamaica

British Library Cataloguing in Publication Data
A catalogue record for this book is available from the British Library

Library of Congress Cataloging in Publication Data
Burbach, Roger.
  Globalization and postmodern politics : from Zapatistas to high-tech
robber barons / Roger Burbach with Fiona Jeffries and William I. Robinson.
     p. cm.
Includes bibliographical references.
  ISBN 0–7453–1650–6 (hardback) — ISBN 0–7453–1649–2 (pbk.)
     1. Political development. 2. Postmodernism—Political aspects. 3.
Government, Resistance to. 4. Elite (Social sciences) 5. Globalization. 6.
Ejército Zapatista de Liberación Nacional (Mexico)
I. Jeffries, Fiona. II. Robinson, William I. III. Title.
     JC489 .B87 2001
     327.1—dc21
                                                              00–009741

Cataloguing in Publication Data (University of the West Indies Library – Mona)
Burbach, Roger.
  Globalization and postmodern politics : from Zapatistas to high-tech
robber barons / Roger Burbach ; with William I. Robinson and Fiona Jeffries.
     p. cm.
Includes bibliographical references.
  ISBN 976 95047 7 7 (A r a w a k publications)
     1. Globalization. 2. Ejército Zapatista de Liberación Nacional (Mexico). 3.
Postmodernism—Political aspects. 4. Government, resistance to. 5. Post-
communism. I. Robinson, William I. II. Jeffries, Fiona. III. Title.

     JZ1310.B87 2001   327.1 27

ISBN 0 7453 1650 6 hardback (Pluto Press)
ISBN 0 7453 1649 2 paperback (Pluto Press)
ISBN 976 95047 7 7 (Arawak publications)

10   09   08   07   06   05   04   03   02   01
10   9   8   7   6   5   4   3   2   1

Designed and produced for Pluto Press by Chase Publishing Services
Typeset from disk by Stanford DTP Services, Northampton
Printed in the European Union by TJ International, Padstow

Contents

List of Abbreviations

AFL-CIO	American Federation of Labor-Confederation of Industrial Organizations
ANCIEZ	Spanish acronym for National Independent Campesino Alliance Emiliano Zapata
ASEA	Association for Social and Economic Analysis
CAFOD	Catholic Agency for Overseas Development
CIOAC	Spanish acronym for Independent Center for Agricultural Workers and Peasants
CNC	Spanish acronym for National Confederation of Campesinos
CONAIE	Spanish acronym for Indigenous Nationalities Confederation of Ecuador
ESOP	Employee Stock Ownership Plan
EZLN	Spanish acronym for Zapatista National Liberation Army
FDI	Foreign Direct Investment
FPEI	Foreign Portfolio Equity Investment
GOP	Grand Old Party (US Republican Party)
ILO	International Labor Organization
IMF	International Monetary Fund
IWW	International Workers of the World
NACLA	North American Congress on Latin America
NAFTA	North American Free Trade Agreement
OECD	Organization for Economic Cooperation and Development
OSCE	Organization for Security and Cooperation in Europe
PGA	People's Global Action
PRI	Institutional Revolutionary Party
SAPs	Structural Adjustment Policies
SPD	German acronym for Social Democratic Party
UCLA	University of California at Los Angeles
UNCTAD	United Nations Conference on Trade and Development
WTO	World Trade Organization

Acknowledgements

Many people have helped me as I traveled, researched and wrote the different parts of this book over the past half dozen years. My early writings on the Zapatistas are the result of my participation in a delegation to Chiapas organized by Medea Benjamin of Global Exchange that took place a few months after the Zapatista uprising in early 1994. Ben Clarke, a member of the delegation, was especially helpful in getting me around in my wheelchair as I got on and off buses, went through military checkpoints, and even had the good fortune to visit the Palenque ruins in Chiapas. In these early years Raymond Barglow was also very helpful in going over some of my initial writings and ideas on globalization.

Peter Rosset and Food First pushed my early work along by encouraging me to write an article on the history of capitalist agricultural development in the state of Chiapas. Carmen Diana Deere and Jack Amariglio helped arrange my participation in the Conference on Politics and Languages of Contemporary Marxism at the University of Massachusetts in Amherst in 1996. They, along with David Ruccio, the editor of an article of mine that appeared in *Rethinking Marxism*, helped me develop some of my ideas on the relationship between Marxism and postmodernism that are found in this book. I would also like to thank Fred Rosen for asking me to write an essay for NACLA on socialism in the Americas. That essay, along with his comments and suggestions, are a central part of the chapter on socialism and postmodern politics in Latin America.

In late 1997 I visited Nicaragua where I discussed many of the ideas of this book with my old friend, Orlando Nunez. He as usual provided critical insights that helped me sharpen many of the concepts presented in the pages that follow. Carlos Fernando Chamorro, another comrade from Nicaragua, kept challenging me with his thoughts and ideas, particularly while he was teaching in the journalism school at the University of California in Berkeley.

Throughout the process of writing this book my good friends Karen Judd, Robert Armstrong and Hank Frundt provided me with personal and intellectual support. Glenn and Marilyn Borchardt also gave freely of their time, particularly over extended dinner conversations at their home. Glenn was also very helpful with his expertise on word processing. My sister Miriam Burbach provided her usual personal support during the course of writing this book. She put me up in her house and helped with the logistics of participating in the "Battle of Seattle" in late 1999, which shaped the introduction for this book. And I would like to thank Cathy Schneider for sharing her apartment and her ideas on the state of the world while I participated in the "Battle of Washington D.C." in April 2000.

David Parkhurst provided the technical support for me to master the information age with my laptop computer. He also tried to get me to present my ideas on postmodernism in a more accessible form. Fred Goff of the Data Exchange in Oakland was always willing to help with specific research requests. Michael Watts of the University of California at Berkeley arranged for my appointment as Visiting Scholar at the Institute of International Studies, enabling me to tap into the research facilities of the university.

The comments of my editor at Pluto Press, Roger van Zwanenberg, were invaluable in compelling me to refine and develop the ideas for this book. I would also like to thank Bill Robinson and Fiona Jeffries for their collaboration in writing several chapters. Aside from their chapters, the concepts and ideas presented in the rest of the book are my responsibility alone.

Thanks for support or help in one form or another from Kevin Danaher, Eric Leenson, Cecile Earle, Monica Marini, Paul Chin, Sharon Pastori, Elizabeth Farnsworth, Dr Miciyo Kawachi, Patricia Flynn, Fiona Dove, Carol Berstein Ferry, Walden Bello, Anuradha Mittal, Antonio Prieto, Paul Rice, Diana Bohn, Claudio Duran, Peter Utting, Amalia Chamorro, Hermione Harris, Susan Browne, Dick Walker, Peter Waterman, Melissa Tuggle, Elias Padilla, Judith Brister, Susan Meiselas, Lea Guido and Ileana Rose Marie Pisano. Finally, thanks to Tim Draimin for his last-minute help and to Mohamed El-Doufani for his editorial work.

The support and accompaniment of my two children, Matthew and Alexandra helped me survive the challenges of writing this book. It has been especially heartening to see my son reach intellectual maturity and show an active interest in discussing some of the drafts and ideas presented here. This book is dedicated to the new generation of global activists who are intent on transforming the world they inherited from the century past.

Introduction:
Globalization, New Resistances and the Postmodern Age

In the waning days of the old millennium, tens of thousands of demonstrators gathered in the city of Seattle to protest the meetings of the World Trade Organization (WTO). They held workshops and forums, staged marches, occupied the streets of downtown Seattle and blockaded the entrances to the WTO gatherings. The demonstrators called for "fair trade, not free trade," and an end to the "new tyranny" of the WTO, an organization they denounced as a front for multinational corporations and "profits uber alles." As a French farmer in Seattle who had previously pulled off the roof of a McDonald's restaurant in France with his tractor proclaimed, "resistance, resistance, and resistance, that is the only way to stop this global machine from consuming and destroying our ways of life."

Why did the WTO, an organization barely five years old, provoke the Battle of Seattle? For many from around the world the WTO had come to symbolize the tremendous damage being done by globalization. In Seattle, U.S. and Canadian farmers along with South Korean rice growers and Caribbean banana farmers demanded an end to a trade regime that squeezes out small producers while favoring large agribusiness firms. Environmentalists of all stripes were also present in Seattle, adamantly opposing the big resource extraction companies that are destroying the world's old growth and rain forests while drastically reducing or killing off thousands of species ranging from turtles and dolphins to the spotted owl and the Monarch butterfly. Marching with environmentalists and farmers in Seattle were trade unionists from such divergent U.S. organizations as the Teamsters, the American Federation of Teachers and the old International Workers of the World (IWW), along with union representatives from Canada, Europe, Latin America, Asia and Africa. They demanded an end to a trade system that allows corporations to scour the world for cheap labor, driving down living standards and undermining hard won social victories in rich and poor countries alike.

1

The Battle of Seattle reflects the core issues that are taken up in this book—globalization, the crisis of the left and postmodernism. Globalization, meaning the internationalization of economies and societies, has integrated the planet as never before under the dominance of multinational corporations. Simultaneously, globalization has adversely impacted living standards around the world, shattering local cultures and societies, fomenting a new type of oppositional politics. As Dan Seligman of the Sierra Club commented in Seattle: "The things people believe in are less secure. Their communities are more fragile ... And people are beginning to connect that to corporate power, media control, and politics stacked against them."[1]

It is this fragmentation, insecurity and dramatic upheaval caused by globalization that have eviscerated the traditional left and created what can be called a postmodern political age. The established political parties were largely absent in the streets of Seattle. Present was a potpourri of organizations with no singular political platform or philosophy. The political ideologies, or metanarratives, that drove the politics of the twentieth century were largely irrelevant, as organizations as diverse as the Sierra Club, the Direct Action Network, the National Family Farm Coalition, the Humane Society, the AFL-CIO, Earth First and Global Action cooperated in organizing many of the marches and demonstrations that challenged the WTO. Politics in the postmodern age is "de-centered," with a wide variety of groups coming together on any given issue to challenge the established order.

William Greider, drawing on the imagery of environmentalists dressed as turtles marching with trade unionists, commented on the sea change in politics that emerged in Seattle:

> The corporate-political establishment doesn't get it yet, but sea turtles and Teamsters (with their myriad friends) can change the world. This popular mobilization, disparaged as "Luddite wackos" by the prestige press, is still inventing itself, still vulnerable to the usual forces that can derail new social movements. But its moment is here, a rare opportunity to educate and agitate on behalf of common human values.[2]

THE LONG AND BLOODY MARCH OF GLOBALIZATION

To understand globalization, the crisis of the old political order and the new postmodern age it is necessary to take a step back into the past, to see how the triumph of globalization and its ideological talon, neo-liberalism, occurred only after years of conflict, violence and economic aggression. Much of the twentieth century is dominated by the clash between the ideologies of capitalism and socialism. While this was a conflict between two metanarratives with their roots in the Enlightenment, the socialist orientation, at least in its quest for change before taking power, tended to identify with the struggle to liberate societies and nations from oppression. It is this liberating tendency that the capitalist world, led principally by the United States, continually tried to repress and destroy in order to impose its model on the rest of the world.

It is often forgotten that just a short time ago socialism and third world revolutionary movements, rather than Western capitalism, had an air of inevitability.[3] In the 1960s and 1970s the consolidation of the Cuban revolution, the rise of revolutionary struggles in much of Latin America, the stunning defeat of the United States in southeast Asia, the installation of national liberation governments in the Portuguese colonies of Africa, the overthrow of the Shah in Iran, and the victory of the Sandinistas in Nicaragua numbered among the more critical setbacks experienced by the United States and its allies.

But the empire struck back with violence and impunity. Even where it did not achieve outright victory, it so weakened the revolutionary societies through military and economic aggression that by the 1990s they effectively ceased to be viable alternatives. In South America, the victory of the U.S. against all major challenges was already complete by the mid-1970s. The elected Socialist government of Salvador Allende in Chile was violently overthrown in 1973, and by 1976 nationalist governments and revolutionary movements throughout the southern cone had been crushed as three-quarters of the continent's population fell under the rule of U.S.-backed military regimes.

With the victory of the Sandinistas in 1979, Central America became the new battleground. With hindsight it is little short of astounding that this region, so historically dominated by the United States and with a population of only about 20 million, became a critical arena of revolutionary struggle in the 1980s. In an effort to crush these movements, U.S.-supported regimes, particularly in Guatemala, El Salvador and Honduras, along with the CIA-backed contra army in Nicaragua, waged a brutal war against the revolutionary movements, killing well over 100,000 innocent civilians.

And to insure that its fiat was accepted throughout the Caribbean basin, the U.S. invaded Grenada in 1983 and Panama in 1989.

In the case of the Soviet Union and the eastern bloc countries, the collapse of communism is most often attributed to the superiority of capitalism, particularly its late twentieth century "globalization" variant with its free markets and technology-driven economies. It is certainly true that by the 1980s the Socialist bloc countries had come up second best in their competition with the Western world over which modernist project could produce the largest quantity of material commodities. But, as the guardians of the Reagan legacy assert, the Soviet Union was beaten not simply in the economic arena, but also through Reagan's decision to challenge it on the military front with an accelerated arms race. Just as the Soviet Union under Andropov and Gorbachev was beginning to experiment with new economic and political freedoms, the U.S. embarked on a renewed arms race. Even in the United States accelerated military spending in the 1980s placed enormous strains on the U.S. budget and economy; in the case of the Soviet Union, efforts to compete drained away critical resources and helped make the reformist programs of the Soviet leadership unviable, fueling black markets and a growing scarcity of consumer goods.

GLOBALIZATION AND THE WASHINGTON CONSENSUS

Even before the collapse of the Soviet Union, the very nature of U.S. and Western intervention began to shift with the rise of a new global economic order. While much of the third world was suffering from the trauma of imperial interventions in the late 1970s and 1980s, international financial institutions such as the International Monetary Fund and the World Bank started playing more prominent roles in compelling third world countries to open up their economies to international interests. The new approach was embodied in the so-called Structural Adjustment Policies, or SAPs. Countries in financial crisis were granted IMF loans and backing in exchange for severe cuts in social programs, the privatization of public enterprises, and in general, the opening up of their economies to foreign interests. Some of the first SAPs were imposed on Latin American countries in the early 1980s, leading to what some economists have called the "lost decade" of development. By 1990, the average per capita income of the Latin American and Caribbean countries had fallen to 1977 levels.[4]

SAP programs also become widespread in much of Africa and Asia. Even eastern European countries like Poland, while still part of the Soviet bloc in the 1980s, had negotiated economic loans and accords with the IMF and other international financial institutions. While it was generally not recognized at the time, the initial steps of the globalization process were being driven by the efforts of these international institutions to open up markets and impose a neo-liberal economic agenda as part of what became known as the "Washington Consensus."

As the international agencies assumed increasing importance, the United States as the hegemon of the capitalist world embarked on a new foreign policy. Beginning in the mid-1980s the United States came to realize that many of the dictatorships established during the Cold War were no longer viable. Dictatorial regimes, of the right as well as the left, tended to exercise forms of authority over their societies and economies that were increasingly anathema to global capital. The expansion of Western interests required not only open international markets, but also pliable political institutions. Accordingly, the United States shifted to a strategy of supporting what some call "low intensity," or controlled democracies. This explains why the United States abandoned Ferdinand Marcos in the Philippines, Augusto Pinochet in Chile and "Baby Doc" Duvalier in Haiti, seeking to replace them with conservative or moderate governments that would accept the regime of international capital while containing social and political movements that advocated radical or nationalist policies.

In the 1990s the spread of these controlled democracies proceeded hand in hand with the ascendancy of international financial institutions and the consolidation of the globalization agenda. The governments of Mobutu in Zaire and Suharto in Indonesia were allowed to fall largely because they were viewed as "crony capitalists," that is, they had used their access to international markets and international monies to accumulate large personal fortunes for themselves, their families and political associates. The fate of the governments that replaced them was dictated in large part by the way they reacted to Western and global interests. In the case of Zaire, now the Democratic Republic of Congo, the triumphant guerrilla leader, Laurent Kabila, initially refused to accept the political and financial terms the Western governments insisted upon in return for their support. This rejection was key to his inability to create a stable government in central Africa.

In Indonesia, Suharto's hand-picked successor, Jusuf Habibie, at first enjoyed backing from the big powers and international capital but they pulled back when his government became caught up in a major banking scandal. His successor, Abdurrahman Wahid, chosen by a special electoral assembly in October 1999, was immediately placed on notice that it was not enough for him simply to be more democratic than his predecessors. As the *New York Times* noted in its international business section, the "new Government is getting a skeptical reception from a constituency that does not vote but could play a determining role in the future—foreign investors."[5]

This initial skepticism occurred even though President Wahid declared in his first public speech that the two most important words for the Indonesian economy were "foreign investment."[6] What apparently worried investors most was that his economics minister, Kwik Kian Gie, a member of Indonesia's ethnic Chinese business community, might fix the country's exchange rate, which would adversely affect foreign capital while spurring domestic investment, consumption and employment.

THE METAMORPHOSIS OF SOCIAL DEMOCRACY

While the new tyranny of international capital was felt most severely in the third world and the former Socialist bloc countries, the rise of the new global order also had major consequences for the economic and political structures of the dominant powers. During the Cold War era, the Democratic Party of the United States and the social democratic parties of Europe were the principal architects of the welfare state, establishing an array of social programs that provided for expanded education, health care, retirement and unemployment benefits. Full employment was an economic priority and fiscal policies were designed to realize this objective. The platforms of most social democratic parties explicitly stated that their goal was to control and regulate the excesses of the capitalist market, while some, like the Labour Party of Great Britain, even advocated the eventual public control and ownership of the means of production.

The efforts of the Thatcher government in Great Britain and the Reagan administration in the U.S. to dismantle the welfare state were initially viewed as aberrations by many liberals and social democrats who believed that attacks on these policies would provoke a public reaction. But the offensives against these social programs along with the drive for "deregulation"—meaning the elimination of many labor rights and the striking down of public interest laws that regulated businesses—were part of a more fundamental shift that occurred as finance capital began to exert a more decisive influence over state policies. With the growth of international monetary markets, the value of national currencies and interest rates became increasingly susceptible to the whims of international finance capital. This meant that governments began to lose control over their budgetary and social policy options.

Here the early years of the Socialist government of François Mitterand in France illustrate what was happening. Mitterand became president in 1981 on a platform of higher wages and an expansion of the state sector, including increased public ownership and control of the country's banking system. These policies were anathema to local and international capital. A run began on the franc, thereby depreciating the French currency and driving up interest rates. This in turn meant higher payments on the French national debt, rising inflation, and a "strike" by private investors as they refused to invest in the French economy.

Faced with this deteriorating economic situation, Mitterand did an about face and abandoned the Socialist Party program, freezing wages, cutting public spending and even curtailing welfare programs. "Confidence" in the French economy eventually returned as international investors stopped disinvesting, and economic growth resumed. Mitterand was re-elected in 1988 and remained in power until 1995, but his economic policies differed only marginally from those of more conservative governments in Europe as the government even began privatizing some state enterprises, like the automotive company Renault, which had been under state control for decades.

This pattern was repeated in myriad ways throughout western Europe in the 1980s and 1990s. The Swedish social welfare state, the most efficient and progressive in the Western world with control over 60 per cent of the country's GDP, also came under attack in the 1980s. In this case, the ruling Swedish Social Democratic Party began to undermine the public sector in the mid-1980s by deregulating the financial markets and abolishing exchange controls. Next the party cut the progressive tax system, turning to a more regressive VAT or sales tax, and then in 1990 it passed an austerity package that froze wages and banned strikes for two years. This led to a rise in unemployment, and in 1991 the Social Democrats lost power to a conservative coalition that deepened the assault on the Swedish welfare state. Returned to office in 1994, the Swedish Social Democrats endorsed the "ongoing internationalisation of the economy," ushered Sweden into the European Economic Community and adopted additional economic measures that limited the state's ability to control social and fiscal policies.[7]

It is the growing power of finance capital in the context of globalization that explains why Bill Clinton in the United States and Tony Blair in Great Britain largely abandoned the liberal and progressive traditions of their parties, advocating policies that largely conformed to a neo-liberal framework. The conscious use of the terms "New Labour" and "new Democrats" reflects the realignment of their parties in a pro-business direction. Early on in his first administration Clinton proclaimed that his foreign policy was guided by the promotion of "free market democracies." In pursuit of these objectives, he pushed legislation setting up the North American Free Trade Agreement (NAFTA) and the WTO, and used the power of the executive branch to support the expansion of corporate interests abroad. Blair, even before he took office, gutted the pro-socialist clauses of the Labour Party platform. And, as one of his first acts as prime minister, he turned the Bank of England into an autonomous entity, allowing it to set interest rates independently of the government, thereby enabling the bank to collaborate more closely with the regime of international finance capital.

While it is important to point out the neo-liberal and pro-corporate tendencies of these leaders, the collapse of liberal and traditional social democratic alternatives should not be personalized or viewed as a simple betrayal. The progressive policy options once pursued by their parties have been trumped by the process of globalization under the auspices of international capital and the array of financial and economic institutions that sustain and reinforce its interests. Any government that tries to break out of this framework is "disciplined" and brought to its knees.

OLD AND NEW POLITICS

Democracy may now be the catch phrase for modern societies, but it is a hierarchical democracy in which the gulf between the rich and the poor continues to widen. According to a *United Nations Development Report* released in 1999, the richest 20 per cent of the world's population accounts for 86 per cent of total consumption while the poorest 20 per cent receives a mere 1.3 per cent. The assets of the three richest people in the world are equal to the combined GDP of the 48 poorest countries. By 1999, over 200 million more people lived in abject poverty (less than a dollar a day) than a decade before.[8]

Gone is the old historic alternative in which governments and nations broke out of the capitalist system by adopting command economies that limited or eliminated the role of foreign and private capital. This was the "modernizing" path followed by the socialist and communist parties when they came to power in the twentieth century, and it has been largely discredited with the collapse of the Socialist bloc. Only the remnants of a few old political formations and left-wing intellectuals continue to advocate this approach. For the overwhelming bulk of the world's population, socialism "as we knew it" has no appeal. It is no longer functional and cannot be resurrected.

This does not negate the reality that there is enormous discontent, and even outright rebellion, against the reign of international capital and the policies of its subservient governments around the world. The uprising of the Zapatistas in Mexico in 1994, the strikes and mass demonstrations of French workers and farmers in the mid-to-late 1990s, and the innumerable campaigns of activists around the world, like those demanding an end to the marketing of genetically-altered foods and the Jubilee 2000 campaign calling for a canceling of the debt imposed on the poor countries—these are but a few of the on-going resistances to neo-liberalism and corporate-financial interests. Victories were even won by the opponents of globalization in the 1990s with the derailing of the Multilateral Investment Accord and the defeat of legislation in the U.S. that would have expanded NAFTA. And the massive protest demonstrations in Seattle as the World Trade Organization met—which were a critical factor in derailing a new round of trade agreements by the WTO—showed that opposition to the new global order was alive and well in the waning days of the twentieth century.

What is notable about all these resistances is that they are not taking place under the leadership of political parties, be they liberal, social democratic or communist. Most of these parties are no longer relevant or able to facilitate change because they have been discredited, destroyed, or have fallen under the sway of international capital. Due to the compromised state of political parties and leaders, traditional politics is increasingly viewed as a spurious arena of activity by large swaths of the globe's population, especially by the youth, which has become apolitical or practices a new "anti-politics." It is no surprise that in Seattle the contingent that turned to violence was a group of very young anarchists from Oregon who proclaimed "it's time to create a new world from the ashes of the ruined one."[9] The Direct Action Network, a much larger organization that mobilized thousands to come to Seattle and, unlike the anarchists, practises non-violent civil disobedience, also draws heavily on a younger generation that is estranged from traditional politics.

This growing alienation is part of the more general crisis of modern political systems that can only be understood from a postmodern perspective. Virtually all political parties, including those on the left, are steeped in modernity and are heirs of the Enlightenment project. Donald Sassoon in his promethean tome, *One Hundred Years of Socialism*, repeatedly refers to the socialist projects as being all about modernity and "modernization."[10] These parties ardently believed that they could raise up the masses, giving them access to the cornucopia of goods offered by modernization and materialism by seizing and exercising state power, either through the ballot box or by carrying out a revolution. Today this strategy has reached a dead end.

By failing to recognize that there has been a fundamental shift with globalization and that the very conceits of modernity need to be questioned, all the old variants of the left are in effect locked into the logic of the neo-liberal world. Here they would do well to take up the challenges presented by John Gray's *False Dawn: The Delusions of Global Capitalism*. A late-modernist critique of how neo-liberalism constitutes the final act in the wider malady of rationalist utopian thinking that began with the Enlightenment, Gray argues that globalization, the concrete expression of neo-liberalism, is destined to self destruct just as socialism did. He points to the experiences of social democratic governments in New Zealand and Australia to demonstrate how the Keynesian welfare state is unraveling in a laissez faire, globalized world.

Gray's basic prognosis is one of failure for the universal free market as the new utopia. He totally rejects Fukuyama's thesis that the triumph of democratic capitalism over socialism represents the "end of history." The laissez faire capitalism that drives globalization is actually incompatible with authentic democracy. "The free market does not promote stability or democracy," declares Gray.[11] He goes on to point out that globalization is destroying the foundations of social cohesion around the world, and that ethnic wars are merely part of the growing chaos and disorder that are being fomented as laissez faire capitalism imposes itself on the globe. The final paragraph of *False Dawn* proclaims: "we must expect that the global free market will shortly belong to an irrecoverable past. Like other twentieth-century utopias, global laissez-faire—together with its casualties—will be swallowed into the memory hole of history."[12]

While Gray sees "alternative capitalisms," such as the emerging system in China or the Japanese model, as possessing cultural and economic attributes that could challenge the universalist values of laissez faire globalization, he does not present any fundamentally different alternatives to neo-liberalism and capitalism as the final expression of rationalism and the Enlightenment. But the real world, given all its fragmentation and incoherence, is resisting the capitalist global order in many different ways and continually searching for alternatives. Sustained and continual opposition to the hegemony of the new global order comes from rebellious factions that appear anywhere and everywhere, as the Battle of Seattle demonstrated. The opposition is postmodern in the sense that it has no clear rationale or logic to its activities while it instinctively recognizes that it cannot be effective by working through a "modern" political party, or by taking state power. It functions from below as an almost permanent rebellion, placing continuous demands on all the powers that be.

At the beginning of the new millennium there is not a new paradigm or metanarrative capable of giving us direction or a world view. But there are new perspectives, many of which trace their origins back to the counterculture of the 1960s that questioned traditional values and beliefs. The counterculture activists of that generation may have been naive in many ways, as was their credence in "flower power." But they basically got it right with their rejection of the rules and values that undergird our modern political and economic systems.

We need to recognize that the dominant discourse of the Enlightenment—that we are on a path of inevitable progress under the guidance of science and technology—is no longer functional in terms of advancing human dignity, or ensuring the very survival of the planet. While science and technology certainly can assist the common good, it is the dominance and control of these endeavors by corporate interests and the nation state—whether socialist or capitalist—that have led to systematic abuse and the wanton destruction of life. The twentieth century, which witnessed the most intense application of science and technology in human history, also gave us two major world wars and horrific human carnage extending from Armenia early in the century to the Holocaust, the Gulag, Hiroshima, Rwanda and, lastly, Bosnia and Kosovo.

While propagating fundamental human inequities and genocide, the order of modernity also places human beings on a pedestal above all other forms of life on the planet, controlling and manipulating them at will through the application of science. Modernity does not recognize the true limits of the human condition, that in fact humanity is part of a larger chain of life. The modern nation states, while passing paltry environmental laws, are incapable of breaking with the politics of modernization and economic growth that are integral to the spread of global capitalism and the destruction of the environment.

Many Marxists and those on the intellectual left have repudiated postmodernism because of its relativism and its rejection of political ideologies and metanarratives. Undeniably, there are some currents of postmodernism that wallow in a new nihilism and are obsessed with questions of language and conceits. By directly or indirectly disdaining any activity as meaningless, they reinforce and help sustain the current order. This is especially true in the academic world where some postmodernists, particularly in the fields of anthropology, history and literature, often oppose those who believe that we can engage in study and analysis in order to act and improve our world. In effect these postmodernists represent a new type of dogmatism with their insistence that all efforts to establish any values or to provide leadership can only lead to new tyrannies in which minority views are repressed.

As is shown in Part Two of this book, there are many other currents of postmodernism that can provide us with new perspectives for envisioning a different world. In the effort to overturn modernity, it is not necessary to reject certain ideas that have a long history of being useful and important for human civilization. Some of the oldest Judeo-Christian values, such as "Thou shalt not kill" are de facto universal beliefs; although they assume specific meanings and interpretations in every society, they nonetheless constitute basic building blocks for human communities. In more recent history, the United Nations Declaration of Human Rights is also a broadly articulated vision of basic human values. Although these rights are often adhered to more in word than in deed, it is notable that virtually all the nations of the Earth have endorsed this declaration.

An unintended effect of globalization is that we are becoming more aware of the divergent values, cultures and societies that exist on the planet, many of them non-Western and largely unformed by the Enlightenment. If the human species is to move beyond the authoritarian, universalist projects of the past, then we will need to find new ways to coexist as divergent cultures and societies. Perhaps the Zapatistas have best captured the paradoxes and hopes of the postmodern age with the slogan "one world with room for many worlds."

It is these debates and discussions over postmodernism, modernity and globalization that are taken up in the rest of this book. The chapters presented here deconstruct globalization while discussing the new social activitists and movements that are striving to move beyond the politics of modernity. While the years since the collapse of socialism have raised more questions than ever about the viability of the neo-liberal project, the traditional left as a political force has not been able to take advantage of these openings in any significant way. It is in deep crisis, particularly on the ideological level, and will remain so until it deals with the legacy of three centuries of modernity.

The first published article included in this book (Chapter 8), which originally appeared in *New Left Review*, is about the origins of the Zapatista movement in Chiapas, Mexico.[13] Since the uprising on January 1, 1994, the Zapatistas have come to embody a new approach to revolutionary struggle, one based on the transforma-tion of civil society, not on the simple seizure of state power. This is an indigenous ethnic movement, and unlike many of the ethnic conflicts in eastern Europe and parts of Africa, it has a progressive, internationalist agenda with links to the ecological and feminist movements and to the remnants of the left in the first and third worlds.

In this article I first raised the concept of postmodernism and its relationship to radical political struggles, portraying the Zapatistas as a postmodern movement because they are resisting the forces of modernity propagated by capitalism. My characterization of the Zapatistas as postmodernist opened up a debate, particularly in the pages of *Monthly Review*, in which I was strongly criticized for supposedly abandoning left and revolutionary politics by embracing a postmodernist perspective.

As this was happening the previous book I co-authored for Pluto Press was published: *Globalization and Its Discontents: The Rise of Postmodern Socialisms*.[14] There I laid out controversial arguments on globalization and postmodern socialisms that have been contested by sectors of what I call the classical left. Regarding globalization, I took the position that it is a new period in capitalism's evolution, while I used the term postmodern socialisms to characterize a new de facto approach on the left, one that roots itself in specific social struggles and strives to change the world from the bottom up without any fixed or preordained political ideologies.

At about the time of the book's release in late 1996, I participated in the Conference on Politics and Languages of Contemporary Marxism at the University of Massachusetts in Amherst. Sponsored by the periodical *Rethinking Marxism*, the conference brought together progressive and left scholars from around the world to discuss new approaches and analyses. Attending also was a dissident faction, which attacked those on the left who tried to use postmodernism to advance a radical perspective.

The conference compelled me to expand and deepen my own thinking on these issues, and I turned my presentation at the conference into an essay, which was published in *Rethinking Marxism*: "The (Un)defining of Postmodern Marxism: On Narrating New Social and Economic Actors."[15] In this essay, which I have substantially revised and turned into Chapters 5 and 6 of this book, I discuss the shortfalls of classical Marxism, particularly the decline of its major protagonist, the proletariat, while pointing to new forces for advancing radical struggles, especially the social movements.

Many of the same classical leftists who are steadfastly against incorporating postmodern concepts into a new left perspective have also come out against the existence of globalization. Their contention is that nothing has fundamentally changed, that capitalism is still capitalism. Capital, they say, has been operating on a global level ever since European expansionism began in the sixteenth century, or at least since the advent of the industrial revolution in the eighteenth century.

This argument led me to work with Bill Robinson on an essay titled "The Fin de Siecle Debate: Globalization as Epochal Shift," published in *Science & Society*.[16] Revised and expanded for this book as the first two chapters, they lay out the fundamental transformations that are occurring in the capitalist world with the internationalization of capital and production. Robinson and I maintain that for the first time in history an international bourgeoisie is beginning to coalesce, and that states and governments, while by no means irrelevant, are being reshaped and restructured so that they can better serve the global interests of the new ruling strata.

The style and content of these first chapters reflect my belief that in the postmodern age it is as important as ever to produce hard hitting analytical articles that some postmodernists may label "essentialist." In particular I hold that open-ended, dialectical reasoning is still a critical tool for helping us to better understand the world. As many postmodernists argue, it is important to "deconstruct" many of the conceits that are employed by academics, intellectuals and others, but this does not mean that we need to abandon clear reasoning and attempts to lay out our core ideas about what is actually transpiring in the world.

While working on the article on globalization, NACLA's *Report on the Americas* asked me to write a 30th-anniversary essay on socialism in Latin America. I saw this as an opportunity to assess what had happened to the left in Latin America during the past 30 years, and to apply a postmodernist perspective to current popular struggles in the region. The resultant essay took a critical look at the Popular Unity government in Chile under Salvador Allende, the New Jewel Movement in Grenada, the Sandinista revolution in Nicaragua, and the Cuban revolution.[17] While the Chilean experiment was essentially democratic, the other three I argue were, to one degree or another, adversely affected by centralist, top-down leadership. It is this authoritarian tendency of past revolutionary movements that contemporary social and political movements in Latin America are trying to overcome.

Chapter 7 expands on this earlier essay on socialism and alternative struggles, looking in particular at peasant, indigenous, and human rights movements in Latin America, showing how they are part of the resistance to globalization. These and other social movements I argue are adopting a more democratic, participatory approach, and are formulating their own popular struggles and perspectives without being driven by a set ideological perspective.

The three remaining chapters were written for this book with an eye to filling in certain gaps in the discussion of globalization, the left and postmodernism. In researching Chapter 4, "Shades of Postmodern Politics", I was struck by how little has been written on postmodernism and politics. Postmodernism itself is a very illusive term, meaning many different things to different people. To help clarify our understanding, I discuss what constitutes postmodern politics and how we need to differentiate between the condition of postmodernity and postmodernism as a philosophy. The chapter also discusses how postmodernism has been appropriated by sectors of the new right as well as the left, especially in Europe. Finally, the chapter turns to several progressive theorists who have critiqued some aspects of postmodernism, while using other postmodernist insights to advance radical, and even socialist struggles.

After revising the first two chapters on globalization, I realized that it was necessary to look at the corporate vanguard of the globalization process, the high-tech entrepreneurs, lauded by much of the media as innovators who are bringing us the cornucopia of the "information age." Chapter 3 critiques this exalted image by looking at the many parallels between this new business class and the Robber Barons who seized control of the U.S. economy at the end of the nineteenth century. These "cyber" barons rival or surpass their predecessors of the Gilded Age in terms of extravagant wealth and pernicious and monopolistic business practices, as well as their exploitation of the "flexible" labor force.

The final chapter, Chapter 9, by Fiona Jeffries, explores how the Zapatistas have used the technologies of the information age to advance popular struggles on the international level. Particular attention is paid to the intergalactic gathering in Chiapas in 1996, and other initiatives of the Zapatistas that make them a very different movement from the earlier national liberation movements of the third world. The Zapatistas's radical democratic approach, and their use of the "digital mirror," demonstrate that it is possible to use the spaces and technologies opened up by globalization and the information age to build new movements and struggles that are simultaneously local and internationalist in scale and scope.

While completing the final draft of the book I went to Seattle to participate in the demonstrations against the World Trade Organization in late 1999. This event, a victory for progressives forces as the WTO talks collapsed, reinforced and advanced my arguments in the book that we are in an age of new politics that can best be understood from a postmodern perspective. I subsequently worked with Kevin Danaher to put together an edited anthology on the events of Seattle, *Globalize This! The Battle Against the World Trade Organization and Corporate Rule*.[18] Parts of the introduction we wrote for that book helped shape the introduction presented here as well as the chapter on the virtually existing global revolution.

The chapters in this book are broken into three parts, the first one focusing on questions of globalization, the second on postmodernism and its relation to politics and the left, and the third on Latin America and the Zapatistas in the postmodern age.

Part One

Globalization

1 The Epochal Shift*

Over the past quarter century the global economy has come to exert an almost transcendental importance in our lives and societies. While the term "globalization" is generally used to describe this transformation, heated controversies abound over the significance and extent of globalization. Not even established economists and defenders of the neo-liberal order agree on how to assess the current era, while liberals, social democrats and those on the left are divided over how to interpret and respond to globalization.[1]

Our position is that globalization marks an entirely new epoch in the world's economic history. As such it requires a shift in our *weltanschauung*, the very way we view the world, its politics, societies and economies. To understand this epochal shift, we need to situate it in relation to other fundamental transformations in the history of capitalism.

First came the age of discovery and conquest. Capitalism, emerging from its feudal cocoon in Europe, began its outward expansion, symbolized by Columbus's arrival in the Americas. This was the epoch of mercantilism and primitive accumulation, what Marx referred to as the "rosy dawn of the era of capitalist production."

Next came the birth of industrial capitalism, the rise of the bourgeoisie, and the forging of the nation state. This epoch spanned what Eric Hobsbawm calls in his seminal historical works the ages of revolution, capital, and empire.[2] It is keynoted by the French revolution and the eighteenth-century manufacturing revolution in England.

The third epoch starts around the turn of the twentieth century with the rise of corporate ("monopoly") capitalism and the financial-industrial corporation, intensified wars among the imperial powers, and the emergence of a socialist alternative. This epochal change is exemplified by World War I and the Bolshevik revolution, the "Age of Extremes," as Hobsbawm titles his history of the twentieth century.[3]

---

* This chapter is based on an article William I. Robinson and I wrote for *Science and Society*, "The Fin de Siecle Debate: Globalizaiton as Epochal Shift," Fall, 1998.

Today we are in the early phases of the fourth epoch of capitalism. Referred to as globalization, it is highlighted technologically by the microchip and the computer—the information age—and politically by the collapse of twentieth-century attempts at socialism. The latter was most graphically signaled by the fall of the Berlin Wall and the disintegration of the Soviet Union shortly thereafter, and also by a lesser discussed event, the defeat of the Sandinistas in Nicaragua in the 1990 elections, which symbolized the failure of a whole generation of third world national liberation movements to offer an alternative to world capitalism.

Periodization is somewhat arbitrary. But we can say that the first epoch ran from 1492 to 1789, the second from 1789 to 1900, and the third from 1900 to the early 1970s. Perhaps the first event that signaled the beginning of the transition to the globalization epoch is when Richard Nixon took the U.S. off the gold standard in 1971. Many have noted that this marked the end of the Bretton Woods currency agreements and the waning of U.S. supremacy. A single headquarters for world capitalism had become untenable as the process of transnational market, financial, and productive integration heightened.

Behind the economic turbulence that ensued in the 1970s was the transition from the nation-state phase of world capitalism and its distinct institutional, organizational, political and regulatory structures to a new, still emerging, transnational phase. Other markers include the formation of the Trilateral Commission in the mid-1970s, which foreshadowed the rise to hegemony of a transnational faction of the bourgeoisie, and a lesser-known event, the Cancun Summit in Mexico in 1982. Then the core capitalist states, led by the U.S., launched the era of global neo-liberalism and began imposing structural adjustment programs on the third world as part of this process.

There is a major current of dissenting voices on the left staking out the position that globalization is not a new epoch. These include some world systems theorists who believe in the continued primacy of the nation state. But the most vocal opponents over the past few years have been some Marxists who insist that globalization is an illusion fostered by the ideologues and pundits of the established order. The basic dynamics of capitalism have not changed in any way, these Marxists argue. Capitalism is still capitalism.[4]

If we break capitalism down into its most fundamental characteristics—the exploitation of labor by capital, commodity production, and the continued expansion of capitalism—then yes nothing has changed. However, to take this view one could argue that nothing has changed since Columbus, or perhaps since the industrial revolution, if one defines the earlier period as mercantile capitalism. As A. Sivanandan has argued in an exchange with Ellen Meiksins Wood: "Doubtless capitalism is capitalism is capitalism, but the failure to distinguish between its different avatars freezes us in modes and forms of struggle which are effete and ineffectual and blinds us to the revolutionary possibilities opened up by information technology."[5]

To be sure, leftist critiques of the concept of globalization are railing out against some very disturbing developments. The process of capitalist globalization is used increasingly to justify the continued dominance of capital. On the one hand, most of the establishment politicians of the world, from Bill Clinton and Tony Blair to Ernesto Zedillo of Mexico and Fernando Henrique Cardoso of Brazil, demand concessions from working classes in the name of "national competitiveness" in the global economy. Transnational capital in this way attempts to reify global capitalism as a reality external to its own agency and interests.

Some on the left, or the former revolutionary left, who feel overwhelmed by the seeming power of global capital and are unable or unwilling to adjust their revolutionary outlook and strategy to fundamentally altered circumstances, conclude that no alternative to global capitalism is currently possible—the TINA syndrome, or "There Is No Alternative." The only "realistic" strategy is to try to negotiate the best deal possible with capitalists and to achieve the best "competitive" reinsertion of each country into the global economy. This position is put forth in its most coherent form by Jorge Castaneda in *Utopia Unarmed*. He believes that the left has to accept "the logic of the market" and limit itself to choosing what type of capitalist system it buys into—neoliberalism, or preferably the "social market" of western Europe or Japan, which he argues can be adapted to Latin America necessities.[6]

In terms of practical politics, the TINA stance has been adopted by current leftist supporters of the British Labour Party. To a greater or lesser extent, this critique also prevails among most social democratic and communist parties in the core and among many of the formerly revolutionary parties in the third world. Its adherents include the socialists and communists who are leading France and Italy respectively into the European Union by providing the type of legitimacy for capitalist restructuring that the right could never accomplish. It also prevails among important groups within the African National Congress and the South African Communist Party, the Workers Party of Brazil, the Democratic Revolutionary Party of Mexico, and the Sandinistas in Nicaragua, to cite some other examples.

But the Marxist critics of globalization do not stop at rejecting these disturbing critiques of the current epoch and the political strategies they bring forth. They dismiss the very notion that something is fundamentally new in the world. And they conflate a justified and vital opposition to the process of capitalist globalization with an unwarranted and increasingly dogmatic opposition to the concept of globalization, as if disarming ourselves intellectually is somehow to our advantage in the fight against capital. The problem with their argument that "capitalism is still capitalism" is less its tautology than its ahistoricism. Its logic writes off as insignificant or illusory earlier epochal transitions in the development of world capitalism, such as from mercantile to competitive manufacturing, and then to "monopoly" corporate capitalism. In this way it precludes from our examination the changing historic conditions under which popular classes may mount resistance and construct alternatives. Here we will argue that the current epochal shift, like the previous ones, profoundly affects the roles of governments and the nation state, the way in which class struggle is conducted and manifests itself, and the very contours of societies and the world views of the populations exposed to capitalism.

To demonstrate some of these changes let us compare and contrast the two most recent epochal shifts—that which occurred around the turn of the twentieth century and that which is unfolding today. First, the most critical difference is the organization of capital. Around the turn of the century it is large-scale capital that takes hold, which some call the system of monopoly capital, and others, like Rudolf Hilferding, have referred to as the triumph of financial-industrial capital.[7] These large enterprises were concentrated in particular core nations, mainly those of western Europe and the United States. In virtually all cases these corporations advanced their interests through their nation states. Perhaps the most well-known example of these developments are the large trusts, particularly in Germany, in which the national government coordinated industrial policy so the corporations in a given area of production could better conquer international markets in the interests of the country with which they identified.

The beginning of the end of this system occurred after World War II when the seeds of globalization were sown. The period from the war on is widely recognized as the era of U.S. supremacy. But what is less discussed is that the global capitalist umbrella established under U.S. supremacy enabled the different national capitals to begin to interpenetrate it. A critical development in this process was the formation of the European Common Market. By merging markets and capital, in a relatively short span of perhaps a decade and a half, the scourge of the innumerable wars fought as a consequence of the competition between national capitals that went back centuries was brought to an end. Today, due to the integration of capital and markets, it is inconceivable that there would be a war among the western Europeans nations. World conflict is no longer based on inter-imperial rivalry but is increasingly between global capital and descendant national factions of dominant groups and ascendant transnational factions.

While many detractors of globalization focus on global trade, and therefore, the *market*, in developing their argument, we believe that the process of globalization is driven by the transnationalization of *production* and the transnationalization of capital ownership. These very processes in turn lead to the rise of a transnationalized bourgeoisie that sits at the apex of the global order.[8] The analyses of world trade are very important, but we need to focus on the production relations that underpin market relations, and in turn, the social forces that drive production relations, so as to identify what is qualitatively new in the current epoch.

THE FACTS ON TRANSNATIONALIZATION OF THE ECONOMY

A critical component in the consolidation of transnational capital is the dramatic increase in the flow of foreign direct investments (FDI) among the nations of the world in the 1980s and 1990s. From 1983 to 1987 the average annual FDI outflows were $76.8 billion, a growth rate of 35 per cent per year.[9] In the early 1990s, a slump occurred due to the global economic downturn that affected most of the core countries, which explains why the annual growth rate was only 4 per cent from 1988 to 1992. By 1993, however, the dramatic increase in FDI flows had resumed led by the banner year of 1995 when the increase was 38 per cent. By contrast, other important international economic indicators showed much more modest increases; for example international trade in 1996 increased by 6.6 per cent while the world's gross domestic product grew by 4.5 per cent (see below).

Table 1.1: Global FDI Outflows 1983–97

(Average annual amount and growth rates for batch years 1983–87 and 1988–92)

Year	Amount (in billion dollars)	% Growth
1983–87	76.8	35
1988–92	208.5	4
1993	225.5	11
1994	230.0	2
1995	317.8	38
1996	347	9

Source: As reported by UNCTAD *World Investment Reports*, 1996, p. 4; UNCTAD, 1997, p. 4.

By 1996, the global FDI stock was valued at $3.2 trillion, with its rate of growth over the previous decade more than double that of gross fixed capital formation throughout the world. Moreover, FDI by no means represents the sum total of international corporate holdings; in 1994 it is estimated that the worldwide assets of corporate foreign affiliates was $8.4 trillion. And as of 1995, some 280,000 affiliates of transnational corporations produced goods and services estimated at $7 trillion, which represents some 25 per cent of total world output (calculated on the basis of UNCTAD *World Investment Report*, 1997, which reports that world output in 1993 was $24 trillion).[10] Small wonder that the United Nations Conference on Trade and Development (UNCTAD) declared in the introduction to its 1997 World Investment Report that we are witnessing the "internationalization of national production systems."[11]

One could argue, however, that this internationalization of production represents only the expansion of national capital, that is, U.S. corporations and investors, for example, could simply be expanding their control of the global economy. But here again the facts and figures belie this interpretation. In 1996, U.S. FDI was $85.4 billion dollars, slightly less than a quarter of the total. Even more important to note is that FDI flows into the United States by foreign corporations were $84.6 billion in 1996.[12] This transnationalization of U.S.-based industries is part of a pattern that began in the early 1980s when foreign corporations, particularly from western Europe and Japan, began to make new investments and to buy up established U.S. companies.

Beyond the issue of the transnationalization of U.S.-based companies, it is important to note that, of the $317 billion in total global FDI outflows in 1995, $229 billion went into mergers and acquisitions. This means that less than one-third of FDI was in new or start-up investments: the remainder was used to buy up other companies across national borders. This data, rather than belying the notion of globalization, indicates, in fact, that the assets of many national enterprises, and those social forces bound up with these enterprises, were "internationalized." In the case of mergers, it meant the integration of capitals from at least two distinct countries. If an acquisition, it meant a given firm incorporated a foreign company with its employees, managers, and "national" interests. In 1995, the purchase of the U.S.-based Marion Merrel Dow pharmaceutical firm by Hoeschst of Germany for $7.1 billion was the largest acquisition while the second largest was the buyout of Hollywood's MCA Studio (which was owned by Sony of Japan) for $5.7 billion by Seagrams of Canada.[13]

As in the previous epoch of national capital, the bulk of direct foreign investment outflows, about 85 per cent, continues to originate from the core, or developed, countries of the world, while about 90 per cent of that comes from what is referred to as the Triad, or the European Union, Japan and the United States.[14] Those who argue that globalization is overstated note that the vast majority of these capital outflows are destined for other core countries. However, it is crucial to place the direction of capital outflows in the context of the restructuring of capital globally and of the historic tendencies underway.

The trend towards concentration became particularly pronounced in the 1970s and early 1980s. During 1986–90, a full 83 per cent of FDI flows were intra-core. This reflected the drive of transnational corporations to firmly implant themselves in the largest markets of the world, thereby deepening the process of the internationalization of production that began earlier with the European Common Market. In this regard, the particular spatial pattern of capital flows and internationalization was a natural outcome of a key aspect of globalization: the *transition from the internationalization to the transnationalization of capital* (on this point, see Robinson 1996: a and b). Transnational capital emerged out of the process of core capitals, as reflected in the trend toward core country concentration at the particular moment in which transnationalization took off (1980s). In fact, in a development largely ignored by opponents of the notion of globalization,[15] by the early 1990s this trend began to reverse, with the third world, or the periphery, once again absorbing an increasing share of FDI, as Table 1.2 shows:

Table 1.2: FDI Inflows, 1981–94

In percentage by region

Region	1981–85	1986–90	1991	1992	1993	1994	1995	1996
Developed Countries	72	83	72	67	63	60	65	60
Developing Countries	28	17	28	33	37	40	35	40

Source: ILO 1996–97:3; UNCTAD, 1997:303.

While it is still too early to predict any sustained reversal of core country concentration of FDI, especially in the light of the Asian economic crisis of 1997, the issue of global capital flows—particularly in FDI—needs to be analyzed against the background of the globalization of production. The global mobility of capital has allowed for the integration around the world of vast chains of production and distribution, the instantaneous movement of values, and the unprecedented concentration and centralization of worldwide economic management, control, and decision-making power in transnational capital. At the same time the global dispersal of the circuits of production and distribution involves the relocation of diverse phases in the process of global capital accumulation to different sites around the world. This is done in accordance with a host of cost and political conditions congenial to accumulation, including pliant and/or cheap labor, and lax regulation and taxation, factors which for historical reasons are disproportionately concentrated in the third world.[16]

Thus, the transition from the internationalization to the transnationalization of capital, which involved in the first instance the horizontal integration of the Triad, is being complemented by

North–South vertical integration. The International Labor Organization (ILO) notes that FDI has "increased sharply, especially to developing countries. The average annual flows have increased more than three-fold since the early 1980s for the world as a whole, while for developing countries it had increased five-fold by 1993." The report goes on to emphasize:

> These increased flows of direct investment have been accompanied by the growth of globally-integrated production systems characterized by the rapid expansion of intra-firm trade in intermediate products and of subcontracting, licensing and franchising arrangements, including new forms of outsourcing of work across national frontiers.[17]

The 40 per cent of FDI flows that went to non-core countries in 1996 constitute a larger portion than the economic output of these countries as a percentage of global economic production. According to the UNCTAD, most of this investment went to Asia and Latin America, which received $81 billion and $39 billion respectively. China led with $40 billion, followed by Brazil and Singapore with around $10 billion each. The ranks of the top ten were rounded out by Indonesia, Mexico, Malaysia, Argentina, Peru, Chile and Colombia in that order.[18]

What is surprising to note is that the developing countries themselves invested $51 billion abroad, thereby reflecting the fact that corporations based in the third world are increasingly an integral and active part of the globalization process. The third world bourgeoisie of countries such as Singapore, South Korea, Taiwan, Brazil, Chile and Mexico are becoming significant players on the international scene. What is happening here is a process of transnational class formation, including the emergence of a transnational bourgeoisie out of national bourgeoisies as national circuits of accumulation become integrated at the global level. In 1996 for the first time two third world companies, Daewoo Corporation of South Korea and Petroleos de Venezuela joined the ranks of the top 100 transnational corporations. By the mid-1990s the internationalization of production by third world-based corporations had become particularly pronounced. The top 50 transnational corporations of the third world augmented their foreign assets by 280 per cent between 1993 and 1995, while those of the top 100 corporations based in the core countries increased by only 30 per cent.[19]

Another important aspect of the internationalization of third world economies is the growing importance of foreign portfolio equity investments (FPEI), which are not counted as FDI flows. These are international investments mainly by stock brokerage firms and mutual funds in foreign stock markets. While FDI invariably involves direct management control, foreign portfolio equity investors are generally interested only in securing an ample return on their investments and exercise virtually no direct role in the company in which they invest. In a certain sense FPEI flows represent a "transnationalization" of capital that is even more pronounced than FDI flows in that they are carried out by an array of investors with origins in a large number of countries.

Many third world countries in the 1990s, as part of the drive to implement neo-liberal, free market policies, have facilitated FPEI inflows by establishing or liberalizing their stock market exchanges. Referred to as "emerging markets," much of the economic volatility of the developing economies in this decade is linked to the rise and fall of foreign equity investments. In 1993, FPEI flows to the developing world reached a high of $45 billion, about two-thirds of the level of direct foreign investments, or FDI. However, the Mexican economic crisis that began in late 1994 caused FPEI flows to plummet by 27 per cent in that year and 2 per cent in 1995.[20]

In 1996, FPEI flows recovered, but the collapse of Thailand's baht currency in 1997 and the economic crisis that spread to other Asian economies caused another shakedown in FPEI flows. It should be recalled that when transnational finance capital pulled out en masse from Mexico following the peso crisis, it did not "go home" to the United States or to any other one country, but dispersed throughout North American, European, and Asian markets in search of new opportunities. Similarly, the Asian economic crisis, rather than leading to a retrenchment to "national" protectionist policies, compelled the Asian countries, including Japan, to open up their economies even more.

The growth of direct and equity investment flows are only one part, albeit a central part, of what is at the heart of the globalization process—the dramatic and growing integration of world capital markets through the commodification of financial instruments. One study finds that the total market value of securities traded in world capital markets tripled between 1980 and 1992 and declares that this was "fostered by the rapid expansion in the world economy in the 1980s."[21] The same study revealed that international gross equity flows doubled between 1986 and 1989, and that in 1991 they were equal to more than one-quarter of the capital in the world capital markets. Aside from equity investments, other components of world capital markets are bond and debt financing as well as derivatives, stock options, warrants and convertibles.

Finally, the transnationalization of capital is reflected in ever-greater trade integration. World trade has grown much faster than output, and this growth, after slowing briefly in the early 1990s as a consequence of the worldwide downturn, picked up again in mid-decade, as the following table indicates:

Table 1.3: Growth of World Trade (Goods and Services) and Growth of Real GDP 1974–95

World Trade Growth in Volume in %	World GDP Annual Average in %
1974–83: 3.1	1974–80: 3.4
1984–89: 6.4	1981–90: 3.2
1990–93: 4.6	1991–93: 1.2
1994: 8.7	1994: 2.9
1995: 7.9	1995: 2.8

Source: ILO 1997:3

The decentralization and concentration of globalized production also drives the growth of intra-firm trade in intermediate products and in services. It is difficult to measure the extent of intra-firm trade due to the way transnational corporations are organized. But at the low end of estimates, the World Bank reported that by the early 1980s intra-firm investment within the largest 350 transnational corporations contributed about 40 per cent of global trade.[22]

In sum, over the past decade trade has increased twice as fast as output, foreign direct investment three times as fast, and cross-border trade in shares ten times as fast.[23] The importance of international transactions in the world markets is reflected by the astounding level of global trading in foreign currencies—over $1 trillion a day by 1995.[24] Transnational finance capital has become the hegemonic faction of capital on a world scale and plays a pivotal role in the globalization process.

A major impetus behind the European Union's establishment of a single currency, in this regard, is the need to facilitate the rising tide of activity in world capital markets without having to resort to the continual buying and selling of national currencies. What this indicates, as we discuss in the next chapter, is not so much that European states are "helpless" in the face of global capital but rather that they are acting *on behalf of* transnational finance capital. Similarly, the plummet of Thailand's currency and the flight of capital from neighboring economies in southeast Asia illustrates just how important currency transactions and the internationalization of capital are in the shaping of national economies; more pointedly, in integrating "national" economies into the emergent global economy.

Several months after the economic crisis erupted, Prime Minister Mahathir of Malaysia, who had wedded his country's economic future to international markets and capital, began to openly denounce the IMF and foreign currency speculators for undermining Malaysia's economy. As a *Business Week* editorial pointed out, "dictator-Prime Minister Mahathir ... having become the incarnation of Malaysia's miracle could not accept that world capital markets could with so much ease sink the currency." His attacks did no good of course; in fact every time he spoke out publicly, even more capital fled the country. *Business Week* reasoned that Mahathir had no choice but to follow the logic of the system he had bought into: "A currency crisis is a wake-up call to bring bad finance, budgets, and unreal projects under control. Mahathir and his cohorts better stop blaming the messenger and get the message."[25]

Moreover, the Asian crisis is leading to a restructuring of many of the region's major corporations and economies that facilitates and advances the consolidation of transnational capital. The *chaebol*, the powerful financial-industrial groups of South Korea, have been compelled to sell off national assets to transnational corporations and at the same time they have forged partnerships with corporations from other areas of the world. In mid-1998, South Korea's top 30 *chaebol* were discussing 200 deals with foreign investors, according to Kim Woo Choong, the head of the Daewoo group. Daewoo itself sold a 40 per cent stake in its Korean Telecom monopoly to foreign investors and offered 50 per cent ownership of factories in eastern Europe and the former Soviet Union to General Motors.[26] Meanwhile, the new upstart cheap computer manufacturer, emachines Inc, based in Irvine, CA, was founded in 1998 by

television monitor maker Korea Data Systems and contract manufacturer TriGem Computer Inc, both Korean firms. By early 1999 it
was fourth among U.S. home-PC makers with a 9.9 per cent market
share.[27] These developments are indicative of the externalization of
Asian capital and its accelerated integration into fully transnationalized circuits.

A CAUTIONARY NOTE: NATION-STATE BIAS OF ECONOMIC DATA

Much of the literature that points to the significant international
flows prior to World War I in order to argue that there is nothing
new about the current epoch misses entirely the qualitative distinction in international flows today. In the earlier period of trade in
national products, economic and political crises meant that a
withdrawal to more autarchic national economies was possible and
also logical. Moreover, as *The Economist* notes, the current period is
very different from pre-1914 on at least three critical counts: 1. large
parts of the world did not participate in the pre-1914 world
economy, whereas the entire world is now integrated; 2. globalization is now driven by plunging communications costs and new
communications and related technologies that facilitate a closer
international integration than in the past and "allow firms to locate
different parts of the production process in different countries"
(hence, globalized production); 3. although net flows of global
capital may be smaller than in the past, gross international financial
flows are much, much bigger.[28]

However, there is an equally important point to be made that
renders such longitudinal comparisons inadequate: the globalization
process itself generates a growing disjuncture between socioecon-
omic phenomena and the way in which we collect and interpret data
on these phenomena.[29]

For instance, some have argued that because only 15 per cent (as
of 1990) of the world's industrial output comes from foreign branch
plants of multinationals, this means that national industrial
production is still overwhelmingly predominant.[30] This covers up
the fact that much of this "national" production is done by transna-
tionals that have global interests and strategies; these transnational
holdings directly shape the way corporations carry on production
and structure social relations in the principal national economy in

which they are based. For instance, Toyota located in a Japanese production zone or Ford located in a U.S. production zone might dedicate a portion of their output for the national market while another, smaller portion is exported. But Toyota and Ford are themselves transnational corporations with integrated international production systems. Therefore, what appears as "U.S."production for the U.S. market and "Japanese" production for the Japanese market is in essence transnational production for specific geographic regions and therefore cannot be conceived as measuring national versus foreign production.

Moreover, the most dynamic corporations are precisely the ones with global investments. They are the wave of the future and sit at the pinnacle of the corporate world. A simple focus on industrial manufacturing and subsidiaries also ignores the growing role of finance capital and world capital markets discussed above, which are the financial motor behind the process of globalization. Among the largest "U.S." corporations, foreign revenues and foreign assets are often 50 per cent or more of total revenue and total assets of these firms. Already in 1991, McDonald's earned more than 45 per cent of its revenue overseas; Boeing, 61 per cent; Colgate-Palmolive, 63 per cent; IBM, 59 per cent; Coca Cola, 64 per cent; Exxon, 78 per cent; Hewlett Packard, 49 per cent; Ford, 39 per cent; Citicorp, 49 per cent; NCR, 55 per cent; Dow Chemical, 51 per cent; Procter and Gamble, 45 per cent; 3M, 49 per cent; and so on. Many of these same corporations employ half or more of their workforce in foreign countries.[31]

Similarly, outsourcing, subcontracting, and intra-firm trade—practices which are expanding rapidly under globalization—conceal the extent of transnationalization by disaggregating and pigeonholing into "national" data sets production chains which are in fact globally integrated. Just as the particular distribution of economic output in the United States among the 50 states, and the ratio of goods marketed within and between states, tells us very little about the nature of the nation state as our object of inquiry, so also aggregate world economic data does not have any inherent meaning in and of itself for global structures. In comparing nation states with transnational structures, we need to focus on the particular fit between sets of institutions, classes and groups, and social production. The problem here is the use of data which itself is collected and registered in nation-state terms to measure a phenomenon that is transnational. In methodological terms, there is a problem of the relationship between theory and fact, or of validity. We are not measuring what we necessarily think we are measuring. Absent a paradigmatic shift away from nation-state centrism in the very way we collect and organize data; it is best to draw qualified conclusions from a broad set of indicators.

THE GLOBALIZATION OF JAPANESE–U.S. CAPITAL RELATIONS

The process of globalization, including the convergence of economic and political phenomena, is further elucidated in a look at the two countries that are allegedly at loggerheads in terms of protecting national capital and national markets—Japan and the United States. Japan, as is widely recognized, has had the most protected markets of the core capitalist powers. Its large corporations have been virtually joined at the hip with the national government, and with one party in particular, the Liberal Democratic Party, overseeing that process.

Changes in the original bone of contention between the U.S. and Japan, the automobile industry, reflect the transition to globalization occurring even in Japan. Japanese automobile firms in the late 1980s began to collaborate with U.S. automobile firms, as exemplified by the joint ventures between Chrysler Motors and Mitsubishi and between General Motors and Suzuki, and by Ford Motors' purchase of a controlling interest in Mazda. In tandem, Japanese automobile firms have internationalized their production, thereby ending their paternal alliance with Japanese workers in which manufacturing jobs were kept at home. Here the building of feeder assembly lines in parts of Asia and the construction of a Honda plant in the U.S. illustrates how Japanese firms have transnationalized their production.

The automobile industry by the 1990s had become, in the words of one researcher, a "transnational spider's web ... stretch[ing] across the globe", in which U.S., European and Japanese automobile firms had become so interpenetrated that national distinctions had lost meaning.[32] A 1993 UNCTAD study reported that transnational automobile companies adopt a strategy of attempting to accentuate the insider-outsider distinction in the U.S. among the government and the public as a public relations strategy aimed at maximizing market shares by influencing a host country public's sense of "who is us."[33] In other words, a transnational automobile company in the U.S. will engage in "Japan-bashing" and generate public perceptions of unfair Japanese practices as tactics of manipulation in its marketing strategy.

The financial and productive internationalization of the Japanese automobile industry explains why Japanese automobile imports to the U.S. are no longer a burning issue in trade talks between the two countries, even though Japanese automobiles continue to be a major component in the ongoing trade deficit between the U.S. and Japan. Since the automobile complex has been at the core of accumulation activities of world capitalism in much of the twentieth century, these recent changes are highly instructive. In the late 1980s, at the height of "Japanese bashing" among U.S. politicians and trade unions over the automobile issue, the ratio of U.S. exports of cars to Europe relative to imports was 1:9, whereas for Japan it was about 1:6.[34] In other words, the U.S. maintained a more unfavorable trade relation in cars with Europe than with Japan.

Applying a nation state-centric framework of analysis, there should have been even greater U.S.–European than U.S.–Japanese trade tensions. But outdated nation state-centric analysis obscures the transnational essence of the phenomenon. The $130 billion merger of Chrysler and Daimler Benz in mid-1998 was merely the most dramatic example of the trans-Atlantic interpenetration of capital that took place from the 1960s onward. It included the interpenetration of U.S. and European automobile firms and also the establishment on both sides of the Atlantic of operations by these transnationalized firms. A similar process between U.S. and Japanese firms, however, did not mature until the 1980s and early 1990s, and once it did, trade tensions lessened in the automobile industry.

In the mid-1990s, the U.S. and Europe pressured Japan to open up its communications system, its financial markets and institutions, and even its shipping and commercial air transport systems. The Asian crisis has accelerated this process, particularly in the financial sphere. The concessions made by Japanese port and shipping interests in October 1997, when the U.S. threatened to block Japanese shipping in U.S. ports, is reflective of the brinkmanship played on both sides as the Japanese are driven to open up their economy. It also shows how states, controlled by transnational factions, push forward the globalization process, modifying economic and social structures in a manner conducive to the deepening of the globalization process.

When these changes are consolidated in shipping as well as other areas of the Japanese economy, there will be a comprehensive inter-linkage of the economies of all the major metropoles of the world. The process of globalization is open-ended and unfinished. But for the first time in history, we can speak of the transnationalization of capital, of a world in which markets are truly global and integrated.

2 Epochal Clashes: Third Worldization and the New Hegemon[*]

The internationalization of capital is making this an epoch of extraordinary conflict, upheaval and uncertainty. Social and class relations are being impacted in virtually every corner of the planet, while the very role of nation states as the dominant institutions for ordering these relations is being challenged. Simultaneously, global capital is striving to put in place an array of supra-national structures capable of ushering in a new era of domination and of disciplining the challenges to its ascendancy.

The volatility of the new global order was brought home in the 1990s by a string of financial crises. First came the Mexican crisis in 1994–95 when the peso collapsed and the country's economy contracted by over 15 per cent. Then in 1997 many of the Asian economies, which had been hailed as third world success stories, suffered a similar fate. South Korea, Thailand, Indonesia, Malaysia and Singapore experienced sharp declines in their currencies and their economic output as capital fled the region. This in turn helped precipitate crises in countries as diverse as Russia and Brazil as global capital pulled out of their stock exchanges and bond markets.

These crises, however, were only the most visible manifestation of the deeper changes being wrought in economies around the globe by the process of globalization. Michel Chossudovsky in *The Globalization of Poverty* contends that the new international regime of capital has had disastrous consequences for the poor:

> The globalization of poverty in the late 20th century is unprecedented in world history. This poverty is not, however, the consequence of a "scarcity" of human and material resources. Rather it is the result of a system of global oversupply predicated on unemployment and the worldwide minimisation of labor costs.[1]

[*] This chapter is based in part on an article William I. Robinson and I wrote for *Science and Society*, "The Fin de Siecle Debate: Globalization as Epochal Shift," Fall, 1998.

Capital Punishment, a special report authored by Duncan Green of CAFOD, a Catholic aid and development agency, declared: "A new challenge confronts the struggle to end world poverty: the growing size and instability of international financial markets." The report goes on to add: "Those countries belonging to what used to be known as the Third World now suffer from heightened and endemic instability, punctuated by frequent currency crises, systemic bank collapses and a disturbing loss of control by governments over their countries' economic destinies."[2]

THE 20–80 SOCIETIES

What is happening is that capital on a global scale is appropriating more and more of the planet's income and wealth while driving down living standards for large swaths of the world's population. Even in the core countries, wages are undermined and the standards of living are under attack. The old breakdown of the world into North–South, core–periphery, or first and third worlds, while still significant, is diminishing in importance. Hans-Peter Martin and Harald Schumann in their book, *The Global Trap*, portray this as the creation of a "20:80 society" in which the top 20 per cent of the globe's population takes more and more of the world's income while the other 80 per cent suffers economic decline or stagnation. As they argue,

> the new International of capital is turning whole countries and social orders upside down ... those who manage the global flows of capital are driving down the wage-levels of their tax-paying employees. Wages as a share of national wealth are declining worldwide; no single nation is capable of resisting the pressure.[3]

The concepts of core and periphery, or North and South, are increasingly not geographic *per se* as much as they are social class in character. The global economy is incessantly churning out new variations, specializations, and asymmetries that cut across nations and regions.[4] Of course, at the turn of the millennium there are still very poor countries and very rich countries. But the trend is one of ever-growing poverty and marginalization in the first world, while the third world has a large number of *nouveau riche* who are able to buy and sell in the global economy, creating vast fortunes that match or rival many in the first world. And in global capitalism's newest playground, the former second world, it is obvious to all that the end of socialism has brought dramatic increases in poverty along with the creation of a new rich and ostentatious upper class. As of 1998, the world's 225 richest individuals with total assets of $311 billion, had a combined wealth of over $1 trillion—equal to the annual income of the poorest 47 per cent of the entire world's population.[5]

The dynamics of globalization suggest that the labor aristocracy that imperialism nurtured in the core countries, as argued by Lenin and other Marxists, might well have been less a feature immanent to world capitalism than an historically transitory phenomenon. The three largest countries in North America that have a free trade zone, or NAFTA, illustrate the trend. The two richest countries—the United States and Canada—have experienced a growing polarization and a decline of the influence of the working classes and trade unions that even adversely affects sectors of their societies referred to as "middle class." Both societies have been "third worldized" to some extent because of increasing marginalization, expanding third world immigration, "downward leveling," and a capitalist strategy of competitiveness through a cheapening and casualization of the work force, all of which are related to the process of globalization.

The United States, with the highest per capita income in the world also has the greatest percentage of its population living in poverty among the industrialized countries.[6] *Pulling Apart*, a study released by the Economic Policy Institute and the Center on Budget and Policy Priorities in Washington D.C. in January 2000, found that between the late 1970s and the end of the 1990s—the very years in which the globalization process gained ascendancy in the U.S. economy—the average real income of the richest fifth of the U.S. population increased by 30 per cent, while that of the lowest fifth dropped by 6 per cent. Even the U.S. economic expansion in the 1990s, with its declining unemployment and tight labor markets, did little to alter this picture as the upper fifth saw its income rise by 15 per cent between 1988 and 1998 while the income of the lowest fifth increased by a mere 1 per cent. Interestingly, New York, the leading financial center of the new global economy, experienced the greatest increase in income inequality of any state between the late 1970s and the late 1990s, while California, the technological heart of the so-called "new economy," numbered among the top five states with the greatest growth in economic disparity.[7]

At the time of the release of *Pulling Apart*, Edward Wolff, author of *Top Heavy: A Study of the Increasing Inequality of Wealth in America* commented:

> Generally what's happening in the U.S. economy is that capital is what's being rewarded, and not labor. Average wages have been stagnant now for almost 25 years, and the share of income going to owners of capital has been rising dramatically in the last 10 years particularly.[8]

This ever-widening gap in the United States is a global phenomenon, affecting rich and poor nations alike. As discussed earlier, parallel to the trans-Atlantic and trans-Pacific integration of capital among the Northern countries there has been an integration of Southern capitalists into the emergent system of transnational capital. The third member of NAFTA, Mexico, illustrates this trend in the third world. Mexico's rich have benefited enormously by pushing for an end to their country's protectionist policies and integrating themselves into the global economy. By the late 1990s, Mexico had 24 billionaires.[9] One of them, Carlos Cabal Peniche, bought up the fresh fruit division of the Del Monte Corporation for more than $500 million. Another one, Carlos Slim Helu, controls Mexico's former state-owned telephone company, TELMEX, and Sanborns, a chain of Mexican restaurants with affiliated retail stores. To create an international network combining retail and telecommunications, he bought Prodigy, the Internet provider, and in January 2000 took over CompUSA a computer retailer that has commercial alliances with Microsoft Corp and SBC Communications.[10] Back in mid-1997, Slim made an initial move into Silicon Valley in California by buying up 4 per cent of Apple Computers stock. This occurred just days before Apple announced an alliance with Microsoft, thereby running Apple's stock value up by more than 25 per cent, and significantly increasing Slim's assets in the same manner that U.S. finance capitalists expand their fortunes by speculating on Mexico's stock exchange.

Other Mexican-based interests are significant players in the transnational arena. Cementos Mexicanos, or CEMEX, has become the world's fourth largest cement producer by acquiring subsidiaries in the United States, Spain, Venezuela, and the Philippines. Vitro, Mexico's largest glass manufacturer, purchased the Anchor Glass Container Corporation, the second largest glass container producer in the U.S. Even the Mexican media industry is getting into the act, as the Mexico City-based media giant Televisa bought Univision in the U.S. and set up a subsidiary in Chile.[11]

Meanwhile, the Mexican working class, the poor and the indigenous sectors continue to suffer from the "readjustment" imposed on Mexico by global capital in the wake of the currency collapse of late 1994, which resulted in a decline of real wages of over 50 per cent. There has been an economic recovery of sorts in Mexico, but this recovery is highly skewed towards the larger export-oriented businesses and selected sectors of the job market. Over 28,000 Mexican small businesses have gone bankrupt since 1994, primarily due to the drop in domestic demand, while about 2 million Mexican jobs have simply disappeared. Nearly three quarters of all Mexico's urban families cannot afford to buy a basic basket of goods. And the situation is even worse in the rural areas of the country.[12]

NEO-LIBERALISM AND THE EPOCH OF GLOBALIZATION

The neo-liberal policies pursued by many of the world's states are central to explaining the growing polarization of wealth and poverty. Neo-liberalism, meaning economic deregulation, reduced taxes and laissez faire markets, was the economic philosophy of a new bloc of social forces that began to take control of national states in the 1980s, as epitomized by the Reagan and Thatcher regimes. However, there were harbingers of this shift in the previous decade. The dictatorship of Augusto Pinochet in Chile actually served as the first laboratory for an experiment in neo-liberal economics in the mid- and late 1970s with its bloody repression of the working class, privatization of state companies, and dismantling of the public health system. In the U.S., the Carter administration represented a transition period, as its economic policies were caught between the old liberal recipes and the drive for more conservative policies that favored emergent global interests. Carter began the deregulation process and instated neo-liberal monetarist policies with the appointment of Paul Volcker as head of the Federal Reserve system.

Neo-liberalism was consolidated as an integral part of the globalization process in the 1990s by democratic and social democratic governments around the world. In the United States, Treasury Secretaries Robert Rubin and Lawrence Summers served as the economic gurus of the Democratic Party, making free trade, globalization and "market democracies" the centerpieces of the Clinton administration's economic policy. As Robert Reich, Clinton's first Secretary of Labor, stated, "from NAFTA to pushing for China's access to the WTO, the Clinton administration went to the mat over free trade with Congress more determinedly than over any other issue during its eight years in office."[13]

In Germany, Social Democratic Chancellor Gerhard Schroeder forced his finance minister, Oskar Lafontaine, to resign just months after taking office over the deregulation of the German economy and the implementation of policies that were favorable to capital and global economic interests. In early 2000 Schroeder consolidated Germany's swing away from the social market to a neo-liberal economic approach by slashing corporate taxes from 40 per cent to 25 per cent and curtailing social welfare expenditures. In Great Britain, Tony Blair's commitment to a neo-liberal, deregulated global economy was revealed early on in his government when he granted the Bank of England autonomy in setting interest rates. Later, his commitment to a pro-business, neo-liberal agenda was starkly revealed by his vicious attacks against fellow Labourite "Red Ken" Livingstone who campaigned for mayor of London on a platform opposing privatization and calling for state funding and regulation of the city's transportation system and other public facilities.

TRANSNATIONAL CLASS FORMATION AND THE TRANSNATIONAL STATE

The adoption of neo-liberal policies by governments that span the political spectrum means that this shift is no historical anomaly. In effect, neo-liberal states are now ascendant, reflecting a new correlation of social forces in the epoch of globalization. To understand this development, we need to comment on the historical development of the state and the nature of the social classes that have shaped it.

The world economy during what can be called the nation-state phase of capitalism, extending from the 1890s to the 1970s, was characterized by national circuits of production linked to the larger system by an international market and financial flows. Class formation proceeded through the nation state. In the core countries in the early part of the twentieth century, local and regional corporations became national corporations. As national markets were consolidated, national bourgeoisies displayed an organic identity of interests vis-à-vis their foreign rivals as displayed in the two world wars. These bourgeoisies turned to their states for international market expansion and war making, to paraphrase Clausewitz and Lenin, as an extension of economic competition by other means.

In the post-World War II period, the worldwide class struggle unfolded through the institutional and organizational logic of the nation-state system. It spawned: 1. in the first world, Keynesian welfare states and rising affluence; 2. in the second world, efforts to construct an alternative system to world capitalism; 3. in the third world, national liberation movements and multi-class development-alist alliances symbolized in Bandung and the Non-Aligned Movement. In this period, national states enjoyed a varying but significant degree of autonomy to intervene in the distribution of income and commodities. Surpluses could be diverted through nation-state institutions.

However, at the same time, the earlier turbulent period in world capitalist development was giving way to an integrated international market. In the post-World War II era, the multinational corporation and internationalized production spawned international class alliances under U.S. supremacy that sustained the capitalist world order. A new global economy began to emerge, gradually auguring in a process of transnational class formation in which social classes were no longer as tightly bound to national territories as they once were. Here the birth of the European economic union was particularly important in quashing old rivalries and ushering in an era of collaboration among the European bourgeoisie and their states.

In the 1970s a struggle began to erupt between different factions of capital. In that decade and in the 1980s incipient transnational-ized factions set out to eclipse national factions in the core capitalist countries of the North and to capture the "commanding heights" of the state. This struggle is key to understanding the adoption of conservative, neo-liberal policies by the Thatcher and Reagan governments that favored transnational corporate and financial interests. In the 1980s and 1990s similar transnational factions in the South, with the backing of the new interests in the North, began to vie for, and in many countries capture state apparatuses, as happened in the leading Latin American countries, like Mexico, Argentina and Brazil. Once in power, these hegemonic transnational factions set about restructuring and deepening the integration of their economies into the global economy.

With the consolidation of globalization, national bourgeoisies are metamorphosing into local (national) contingents of an emergent transnational bourgeoisie. To the extent that local productive apparatuses are integrated into the transnationalization process, the logic of local and global accumulation tends to converge and the earlier rivalries between capitalists no longer take the form of national rivalries. Competition between capitalists and corporations continues, of course, to be as intense as ever. But, given the separation of accumulation from determined territories and the transnational integration of capitalists, competition is now between oligopolist clusters in a transnational environment. The rapid growth of transnational investments, particularly in the telecommunications and the high-tech sectors, illustrate this new pattern of competition.[14]

Global capital interests are now represented in each nation state by in-country representatives, who constitute transnationalized factions of dominant groups. The international class alliances of national bourgeoisies in the post-World War II period have mutated into a transnationalized bourgeoisie in the globalization epoch, and it has now become the hegemonic class faction globally. This de-nationalized bourgeoisie is class conscious, and conscious of its transnationality. At its apex is a managerial elite that controls the levers of global policymaking, and which responds to transnational finance capital as the hegemonic faction of capital on a world scale.

As Manuel Castells notes in his three volume study, *The Information Age*: "The instrumental capacity of the nation-state is decisively undermined by globalization of core economic activities, by globalization of media and electronic communication and by globalization of crime."[15] However, even though the powers of the nation state have been altered by shifting economic realities, there is no reason to assume that when the state managers adjust national economies to the global economy they are doing so because they are compelled to by some "external" (extra-national/global) force: the national–global duality is a mystification. The determinant feature of the current epoch is the supersession of the nation state as the organizing principle of capitalism, and with it, of the inter-state system as the framework of capitalist development.

Related to this, capitalism is undergoing a dramatic new expansion that is more intensive than extensive. The final stage of capitalism's extensive enlargement began with the wave of colonization of the late nineteenth and early twentieth centuries and concluded in the early 1990s with the reincorporation of the former Soviet bloc and third world revolutionary states. Capitalist production relations are replacing what remains of all pre-capitalist relations around the globe. The era of the primitive accumulation of capital is coming to an end. Because the epoch of globalization does not involve the earlier geographic expansions, such as new territorial conquest, its enlargement is not as visible, and is not as linked to the military might of imperial nation states. There is no longer anything external to the system of global capitalism. As the organic and internal linkage between peoples become truly global, the whole set of nation-state institutions is becoming superseded by transnational institutions.

Here there is a straw man argument made by some opponents of the concept of globalization. For example, Linda Weiss, in *The Myth of the Powerless State*, asserts that "globalists have ... overstated the degree of state powerlessness" under globalization.[16] In this construct, reified states are assumed to want to defend the interests of pluralist "citizens" of their countries. Worldwide shifts in the norm of state policy towards neo-liberal fiscal conservatism are accounted for by Weiss by "internal fiscal difficulties" brought on by "decades of troubled growth, recession and falling real income." She argues that it is not "an all powerful global finance" that accounts for this fiscal conservatism but "electorates" that are "increasingly reluctant to sustain tax and spending increases."[17]

In our view, the trend towards neo-liberalism and worldwide fiscal conservatism has little to do with recession and government inability to raise income, since capital could always be taxed. Instead, the trend has to do with the popular classes' inability to force states to redistribute wealth. And the source of the weakening of the popular classes worldwide is precisely the restructuring of capital on a global scale.

Arguments such as that advanced by Weiss are couched in a dualism between "states" and "markets". Instead, we should analyze in a dialectical manner the nature of states and the social forces that congeal in state structures and practices in particular historic periods. "Markets" are the site of material life while states spring from economic relations and represent the institutionalization of social relations of domination. State practices and the very structure of states are negotiated and renegotiated in specific historic periods through changes in the balance of social forces as capitalism develops and classes struggle. The current epoch is not the first time that capital has broken free of reciprocities with labor expressed in state practices. This happened in the late nineteenth century as the epoch of competitive capitalism was coming to an end and monopoly capital was emerging. Newly strengthened ruling classes can quickly constrict state autonomy as they make more intensive use of the state in times of major capitalist restructuring. In the late twentieth century, capital abandoned earlier reciprocities with labor precisely because the process of globalization has allowed it to break free of nation-state constraints.

Governments are undertaking restructuring and serve the needs of transnational capital not simply because they are "powerless" in the face of globalization. A particular historical constellation of social forces now exists that presents an organic social base for neo-liberal restructuring. Here the case of Mexico is once again illuminating as to how this process occurs even in third world countries. When the transnational faction of the Mexican bourgeoisie undertakes neo-liberal restructuring and integration into the global economy, it is not doing so merely because the Mexican government became "powerless" in the face of globalization, but because the interests of this class faction lies in integration into global capitalism. It was the privatization program that allowed the Mexican billionaires mentioned above to emerge and to join the ranks of the transnational bourgeoisie. And the peso crisis might have thrown millions of poor Mexicans into dire straits, but it saved the necks of the Mexican bourgeoisie just as surely as it saved those of its counterparts in the U.S. and elsewhere.

The political processes bound up with this dynamic can confuse observers attuned to a nation-state framework of analysis. For instance, this is what is behind the power struggle within Mexico's ruling party, the PRI. The "dinosaurs" in the power struggle represent the old bourgeoisie and state bureaucrats whose interests lay in Mexico's corporatist-import substitution model of national capitalism. The new "technocrats" are the transnational faction of the Mexican bourgeoisie that captured the party, and the state, with the election in 1988 of Carlos Salinas de Gortari. Since then, this transnationalized faction has implemented neo-liberal structural adjustment, including the accelerated privatization of public spheres (what Marx termed the "alienation of the state") and commodification of non-market spheres. Similar factions have taken power and are thoroughly transforming the vast majority of countries in the world, ranging from Sweden and New Zealand, to India, Brazil, Chile, South Africa, and so on.

Nor should we dismiss the increased structural power transnational capital and its representatives can exercise over the direct power of states, simply to instill discipline or to undermine policies that may emanate from these states when they are captured by national factions of local dominant groups or by subordinate groups. The assertion that transnational social forces impose their structural power over nations and the simultaneous assertion that states, captured by transnational factions, are proactive agents of the globalization process, only appear as contradictory if one abandons dialectics for the Weberian dualist construct of states and markets and the national–global dualism.

For instance, Weiss argues that "catalytic states" are emerging which act directly to promote the internationalization of capital.[18] But this observation, which we agree with fully, hardly counters the concept of globalization, and indeed, in our view, contributes to it. States have always been central to class development, and in the age of globalization they are indispensable to the development of a transnational bourgeoisie. Transnational capital and the transnational bourgeoisie utilize national state apparatuses to create the conditions for global capital accumulation. Moreover, "strong" states will impose adjustment on "weak" states. But class relations underpin this phenomenon, and it is necessary to move beyond state-centric analysis.[19]

GLOBALIZATION AND TRANSNATIONAL HEGEMONY

The Globalization Epoch and its impact on the nation state also calls for an end to the belief that the capitalist world continues to need a hegemonic nation state to impose order. In the early history of capitalism the Genoese and Dutch capitalists exercised this role, then the British, and more recently the U.S. As Giovanni Arrighi, among others, has reminded us, interregnums between the decline of one hegemonic power and the rise of another have been characterized by instability and wars, such as the period between the early and mid-twentieth century when neither Britain nor the U.S. was able to predominate.[20]

Now all that is changing. The transnational bourgeoisie exercises its class power through two channels. One is a dense network of supranational institutions and relationships that increasingly bypass formal states and that should be conceived of as an emergent transnational state that has not yet acquired any centralized institutional form. The other is the utilization of national governments as territorially bound juridical units (the inter-state system), which are transformed into transmission belts and filtering devices, but also into proactive instruments for advancing the agenda of global capitalism.

Nation states will continue to exist and many will be powerful entities, but, instead of serving the "nation", they now increasingly respond to transnational economic interests, particularly those of footloose and entirely deterritorialized finance capitalists and transnational corporations. There will be no single hegemonic power, or even a regional bloc of nations, to replace the U.S. as its relative importance in the global economy declines. Rather, we are witnessing the creation of a number of international economic and political institutions that are attempting to assume the functions that earlier corresponded to a nation-state hegemon.

Among the key global financial institutions imposing order for the capitalist world are the IMF, the World Bank, and the World Trade Organization. As might be expected, the more explicitly political institutions are trailing behind, but certainly the annual meetings of the G-8 play an important role in coordinating the policies of the key capitalist countries, along with the Organization for Economic Cooperation and Development (OECD) and the Organization for Security and Cooperation in Europe (OSCE). The recent expansion of NATO into eastern Europe and the war against Yugoslavia should not be viewed as simply an attempt by the U.S. and the western European nations to expand their interests at Russia's expense, but as an effort by most of the leading powers to have a more extensive multinational military alliance to impose order in Europe and other parts of the world. The United Nations also is a factor in efforts to create a "new world order," as exemplified by the UN-backed war against Iraq and the interventions in Somalia, Bosnia and the Congo.

Hence, global capitalism is organized in a set of institutions. These institutions include: the transnational corporations that own and manage the world's resources and appropriate its wealth; the international financial agencies that impose the conditions necessary for global capital accumulation to take place; the states of the North, and their junior counterparts of the South, that create the global and the local political, administrative, and legal environment that allow the system to function; and the formal and informal transnational elite forums, such as the G-8, the Trilateral Commission, and the World Economic Forum, which develop strategies for the maintenance and reproduction of the system and supervise its overall operation.[21]

However, this is a period of extraordinary conflict and upheaval precisely because we are witnessing a shift from U.S. hegemony to the early stages of the creation of a transnational hegemony through supra-national structures that are still not capable of providing the economic regulation and political conditions for global capitalism to function smoothly. There will be many unforeseen twists and turns in this process. Nor is it necessarily inevitable that a new transnational elite will fully establish its economic and political hegemony. A major economic crisis or collapse could stymie, or even reverse, the process that is underway. Transnational capital currently enjoys an unprecedented structural power over popular classes worldwide, but this is an historic conjuncture and not a fixed feature of the system. Capitalism has always been a violent and unstable system wracked by contradictions. The confidence exuded by the transnational bourgeoisie—with its "end of history" thesis and so on—conceals a fragility in the foundations of the system.

Therefore, the most critical question is what will be the role of the popular classes around the world in this process. It would be too complex to go into here, but globalization has also led to an increasing popular awareness that transnational, rather than merely national, perspectives are necessary to deal with many issues of popular, grassroots concern. The laboring classes in the North and the South have begun to realize that their struggles against the adverse effects of globalization must take on a transnational perspective and that they even need to engage in transnational organizing. Moreover, most of the new social movements, from the women's rights and gay movements to the environmental and indigenous movements, have a transnational perspective and can be characterized in many ways as transnational movements. The Battle of Seattle in late 1999 revealed that all these different social forces are beginning to coalesce and work together in opposition to corporate-dominated institutions like the World Trade Organization. In the long term the question is whether these movements can build a transnational platform to challenge capital and to make the new global economy serve the needs of the many rather than the interests of the rich and powerful as it currently does.

3   High-Tech Robber Barons: Heisting the Information Age

While globalization characterizes our epoch, authors as distinct as Manuel Castells and Alvin Toffler call this the "information age," an age in which technology and the manipulation of knowledge are at the cutting edge of the new global economy.[1] For most of the twentieth century, industries like steel, automobiles, chemicals and petroleum were the most dynamic centers of economic activity. While they remain important, they are being surpassed by information age enterprises such as software suppliers, telecommunications companies, computer manufacturers and online commercial firms.

The epoch of globalization and the information age are completely intertwined. One could not exist without the other. But these two concepts need to be distinguished: globalization by and large refers to the expansion of capital, production and markets on a planetary level while the informational age denotes the technologies that facilitate the globalization process. The two symbiotically feed off each other. The spread of computers, digital technology and new communications networks—critical activities of the information age—provide the basic infrastructure for globalization to occur. At the same time the continued advance of globalization generates an ever-increasing demand for these new technologies.

Fortune magazine, in its commentary on the top 500 corporations in 1998, took note of the rise to prominence of companies linked to the Information Age, or what it calls the "New Economy." The year 1998 "will probably be considered a watershed" proclaimed *Fortune*, "the year when the New Economy fundamentally parted ways with the old and high-tech consolidated its role as the driving force behind the growth of big business." The article went on to point out that in order of revenues, the *Fortune* 500 is still dominated by the likes of General Motors, Mobil and Coca Cola, but these companies are "battling their shrinking top and bottom lines," while challengers "like Microsoft, Dell Computer, Cisco Systems and Sun Micro systems, with their high rates of revenue growth and their stock-option-rich employees" make it clear "that one day the *Fortune* 500 will be theirs."[2]

Similarities abound between the information age and an earlier period of economic history, that of the nineteenth-century robber barons. While today's business magnates have built immense fortunes via the "information highway" and the technological infrastructure related to it, the robber barons of the nineteenth century accumulated their wealth by building a new transportation system—the railroads—and seizing control of many of the emergent industries that were linked up by the rails. The major difference between the two is their economic "playing field;" while the robber barons dominated the U.S. national economy, the new corporate, or "cyber," barons of the information age have their sights set on controlling the markets, resources and assets of the planet.

Matthew Josephson, in his classic study titled *Robber Barons*, describes the "aggressive economic age" of the late nineteenth century. The "barons," "kings" or "empire builders," he writes, were determined "to organize and exploit the resources of a nation upon a gigantic scale, ... to do this only in the name of an uncontrolled appetite for private profit..."[3] The likes of James Hill, Jay Gould and Cornelius Vanderbilt amassed huge fortunes in railroads, while key national industries like steel and petroleum fell under the sway of Andrew Carnegie and John D. Rockefeller.

The dynamic and emergent enterprises of our own aggressive economic age are: computer, communications and Internet firms; media conglomerates; bio-technology corporations; and finance and banking companies. Here we will look at these enterprises and the corporate interests that dominate them, focusing primarily on the United States. While the rise of high-tech firms and research centers is now a global phenomenon, the contours of the corporations of the information age appeared first in the United States and are more readily discernible there.

The information age has thrown up a number of U.S. corporate magnates whose economic appetites are every bit as voracious as those of the earlier robber barons: Bill Gates of Microsoft has control of most of the global market for software operating systems; John Malone, the cable mogul of TCI, has gouged the public, exercising local monopolies and charging exorbitant cable rates to build his business fiefdom; Rupert Murdoch of the Fox media conglomerate has bought out or destroyed local competitors and smashed newspaper unions around the globe; Michael Eisner of Disney World stands over an enormous entertainment empire that inflicts its cultural preferences on the world's populace; and Craig Barrett of the Intel corporation is the tycoon of computer processing chips, controlling over 80 per cent of the global market. Some of these names are not yet as well known as the earlier robber barons, but we are only in the early years of the information age. Josephson's study of the robber barons appeared in 1934, well after the closing decades of the nineteenth century when the original robber barons had consolidated their place in history.

Today, in the midst of the early stages of the information age, shakeouts and new names appear with dizzying frequency. It is impossible to predict which figures will be ascendant and written about 30 years from now. John Malone, for example, has merged his TCI interests with AT&T—becoming its largest individual stockholder—and it remains to be seen if the new head of AT&T, C. Michael Armstrong, will eclipse Malone, or if Malone will try to take over or build a new, separate telecommunications empire.[4]

Another rising mogul indicative of the rapid changes of this age is Michael Karmazin, who took control of CBS a few years after the departure of another tycoon, William Paley. In 1996 Karmazin sold his 42 Infinity radio stations to CBS in exchange for $4.9 billion in CBS stock, making him CBS' largest individual shareholder in a company valued at $26 billion. He was also given operational control of the CBS radio network and quickly moved to take over management of the TV stations. Then on January 1, 1999, Karmazin vaulted into the top position as Chief Executive Officer (CEO) of the CBS Corporation. A ruthless business executive, employees refer to Karmazin as "Mad Mel." He has slashed pension plans at CBS and even castigates employees for minor luncheon expenses. His goal is to boost his assets and those of company shareholders by reinventing network TV, converting CBS from "the least-likely to succeed TV network" into a "hot multimedia growth company."[5]

In September 1999 Karmazin set out to repeat his merger-takeover act, this time by combining with a media magnate from the cable and Hollywood studio worlds, Sumner Redstone of Viacom. Redstone became chairman of the board of Viacom-CBS and "elder statesman" at the age of 76, while Karmazin, at 56, took over as the chief operating officer with access to a war chest of $20 billion to make new acquisitions. The heir apparent to Redstone, Karmazin, has a clause written into the merger agreement that requires over three-quarters of the combined board to approve any move to oust him. Eight of the 18 board members are appointed by CBS, thereby giving Karmazin effective veto power over any power grab by Redstone, who ditched his own anointed successors at Viacom.[6]

The greed, perniciousness, and fortunes of the original robber barons are rivaled, and in some cases surpassed, by the owners and executives of the corporations of the information age. According to *Fortune* magazine, Bill Gates, the richest man in the world, is also the richest man in U.S. history, exceeding even the wealthiest robber baron of the late nineteenth century, John D. Rockefeller, by a factor of 311 to 1.[7]

Business Week, in a special issue titled "Is Greed Good?," surveyed the gargantuan salaries pulled down by today's top corporate officials. Between 1997 and 1998 alone the income of the average CEO—some of whom are also chairmen of the boards of their corporations and own large blocks of shares—increased by 36 per cent, while between 1990 and 1998 the increase was a phenomenal 442 per cent. And it is the CEOs of the information age corporations that are driving these extravagant income and compensation packages: of the 20 highest paid CEOs in the United States, 16 headed corporations involved in information age activities. The top five are all key players in corporations involved in globalization and the information age: Michael Eisner of Walt Disney, Mel Karmazin of CBS, Sanford Weill of Citigroup, Stephen Case of AOL, and Craig Barrett of Intel.[8]

WORKERS IN THE HIGH-TECH INDUSTRY

While the new robber barons have accumulated enormous fortunes, ordinary workers have reaped few of the benefits. In Silicon Valley, the birthplace of the personal computer and the microchip, anti-union policies have characterized most of its leading businesses for years. Robert Noyce, who invented the transistor and was a founder of Intel Corporation in Silicon Valley, declared: "remaining non-union is essential for survival for most of our companies. If we had the work rules that unionized companies have, we'd go out of business. This is a very high priority for management here."[9] High-tech companies in the valley during the past half century have operated in a largely paternalistic fashion, paying relatively low wages while striving to keep the trade unions at bay by providing some benefits.

According to the last U.S. census data of 1990, Santa Clara County, the geographic heart of Silicon Valley, had a median household income higher than any other California county with $54,000, and ranked seventh overall in the United States. However, incomes throughout the valley were highly polarized between the very rich and those trying to survive at the bottom. Thirty-one per cent of the valley workforce had annual incomes under $15,000, hardly a living wage in a county that has one of the highest costs of living in the world. Moreover, incomes were skewed according to race and gender, with the bulk of the workforce comprised of minorities. In the valley, 55.6 per cent of Mexican women and 45.3 per cent of Filipina women earned less than $15,000.[10]

These trends have continued since the census report. A study of labor released in early 1998, *Growing Together, Or Drifting Apart*, declared that "Silicon Valley is experiencing a dramatic growth in income inequality and economic insecurity."[11] The report found that, as of 1996, hourly wages for 75 per cent of the workforce were lower than in 1989, while wages for the bottom quarter had declined by 13 per cent. The ratio of earnings of top corporate executives to production workers in the electronics industry in the valley went from 42 to 1 in 1989 to 220 to 1 in 1996. About 19 per cent of all jobs in the area paid less than the living wage for a single adult, while almost 40 per cent earned too little to keep a single parent and a child out of poverty, and 55 per cent did not earn enough to support a family of four.[12]

In the age of "flexible employment" companies throughout the valley have abolished many permanent jobs and contracted work out to agencies for temporary staff, where they have few or no benefits.[13] Regular employment in major computer companies, like Sun, Hewlett-Packard, and Apple is stagant or declining, while these same companies subcontract for many of their components with manufacturers who pay 30 per cent less to their employees.[14]

Moreover, minorities are virutally excluded from executive and board positions. In early 1999 Jesse Jackson's Rainbow-Push Coalition purchased about $850,000 worth of stock in 51 leading high-tech companies, including Apple, Hewlett-Packard and Microsoft. The move was designed to gain access to stockholder and board meetings to call attention to high-tech's "patterns of exclusion." Of the 51 companies with a total of 384 board members, only 24 were women and five were African American while only one company had an Hispanic on its board.[15]

On the national level, high-tech companies have set the pace in mergers and acquisitions, which inevitably leads to downsizing, or in simple words, the elimination of jobs. Characteristic of this trend is the buyout by AOL in 1999 of Netscape, an Internet browser company based in the Silicon Valley. Immediately after the buyout, AOL, based in Texas, announced that 700 to 1,000 employees would be eliminated, about one-tenth of the labor force of the combined companies.[16]

Before its acquisition of Time Warner, AOL reveled in another tendency of many Internet businesses, that of using free labor to promote and expand their companies. In exchange for free monthly accounts, AOL recruited a large number of volunteers, dubbed "community leaders," to perform many routine tasks—such as answering questions by subscribers, supervising chat rooms and enforcing rules and policies. AOL had more than 10,000 such volunteers, all of them committed to a minimum of four hours a week with many spending much more time on AOL tasks. Before the Time Warner merger, a number of volunteers filed a complaint with the U.S. Labor Department, pointing out the obvious, that many of the jobs they perform are identical to those of paid employees of the company.[17]

Mergers and the use of volunteers aside, downsizing of the labor force is a salient characteristic of corporations related to the information highway and high-tech activities. From 1991 to 1995, IBM slashed 85,000 jobs, AT&T, 83,000, GTE, 17,000, Eastman Kodak, 14,000, Xerox, 10,000, and Pacific Telesis, 10,000.[18] Cutting benefit packages is also commonplace among these giants. In May, 1999, with its earnings at record highs, IBM announced it was phasing out traditional pensions for over 140,000 employees, replacing the pensions with "flexible retirement benefits" that cost the workers $200 million in payments per year.[19]

The elimination of jobs due to new technologies and the slashing of benefits explains in part why the U.S. economy in the late 1990s had high growth rates while incomes were almost stagnant. In the first quarter of 1999, for example, the U.S. economy grew by 4.5 per cent and unemployment was the lowest in years. But the pay and compensation packages of workers in that quarter rose by the smallest percentage since the Department of Labor began maintaining such statistics in 1982.[20]

THE KNOWLEDGE MONOPOLIES

Monopolistic tendencies are prevalent among today's high-tech barons just as they were among their counterparts in the late nineteenth century. However, a critical difference between the barons of the past and those of the information age is the manner in which they create monopolies. At the end of the nineteenth century, the trusts and monopolies were constructed through the concentration of processing or manufacturing activities for commodities and products like steel, farm equipment and petroleum.

Many of today's cyber barons, such as Gates of Microsoft, have carved out monopolies based more on patent claims and the control of knowledge than on the manufacture of specific products. As one intellectual property lawyer noted, the manipulation of knowledge assets by information age corporations "makes the monopolies of the nineteenth century robber barons look like penny-ante operations."[21] In *Owning the Future* Seth Shulman declares that "the current trajectory promises nothing less than an uncontrolled stampede to auction off our technological and cultural heritage, a future of increasing conflict and dissension, and the specter of an ominous descent into a new Dark Age."[22]

In the nineteenth century, patents were usually granted for specific products rather than for particular ideas. Thomas Edison, for example, the greatest inventor of the late nineteenth and early twentieth century, saw most of his patented inventions through to production, be it the light bulb, the phonograph, or the mimeograph. Today, however, patents on ideas and specific areas of knowledge are of particular importance and can have more market value than a final manufactured product. Texas Instruments, for example, has during the past several years garnered a larger portion of its $200 million in yearly profits from patents and winning infringement suits than from selling products.[23]

In 1997, IBM alone was granted 1,724 U.S. patents compared to 1,093 life time patents for Thomas Edison. The corporation's total patents number in the tens of thousands and earn the company almost a billion dollars annually. Dow Chemical Company has set up a separate "intellectual-asset management" group to manage more than 30,000 patents, hoping to enhance its "licensing value stream" from $25 million in 1994 to $125 million by the year 2000.[24]

MONOPOLIZING THE LIFE SCIENCES

The most momentous consequence of the "privatization of knowledge" by corporate interests is in bio-technology and the life sciences. Currently, the big rush is on to map out the complete genetic structure of the human genome. Once it is done, this knowledge will give us the power to alter our gene structure, control diseases, and even to prolong life itself. While some researchers of the genome have openly published their results on the Internet, it is estimated that access to at least 15 per cent of the research completed thus far is restricted by private firms seeking to use their knowledge for private gain.[25]

Private control by three bio-technology companies of research on the staff virus known as staphylococcus aureus is already retarding medical efforts to develop new drugs to stop this deadly infection in humans. Some strains of this staff virus have developed an immunity to even the most powerful antibiotics, and private companies are refusing to turn over their research on the staff genome to public medical research centers to help them develop new drugs. According to John La Montagne, deputy director of the National Institute of Allergy and Infectious Diseases, "without this information we don't have the insights we need ... It's like keeping the map of the city of Washington secret." Dr Olaf Schneewind, a leading investigator of the virus at UCLA, adds that the lack of access to this data has "slowed research by four or five years."[26]

In the agricultural sciences, a handful of corporations are intent on dominating the market for bio-engineered crops. By splicing new DNA strands into selected plants, new seeds can be grown that are resistant to insects and fungus, or new plants can be developed that contain added nutritional value. Monsanto corporation, which sold off its core chemical unit and paid $8 billion to buy up seed companies, is a leader in bio-engineering, particularly with its production of genetically altered soybeans that are resistant to the company's Roundup weed killer, which kills all unaltered vegetation. Not to be outdone, DuPont spent $7.7 billion to take complete control of Pioneer Hi-Bred, the world's largest corn seed company. Pioneer is already the largest player in the sale of bio-engineered corn seeds.[27]

Critics argue that there are a number of potentially devastating consequences of these bio-engineered crops. For one, the creation of uniform seeds threatens crop diversity around the world. Furthermore, the spread of bio-engineered crops resistant to certain insects or weeds could lead to the development of "super" weeds or insects that would have devastating consequences for traditional crops grown in the same region. Miguel Altieri, in a survey of existing studies of the ecological impact of transgenic crops, declares that bio-engineering results in the decline of "genetic diversity by simplifying cropping systems," the transfer of genes to other plants, thereby "creating super weeds," the spread of "new virulent strains of virus," and the rise of new "insect pests" that "develop resistance to crops."[28]

Finally, Altieri argues that there is an "urgent need to challenge the patent system and intellectual property rights" upon which the regime of the bio-technological corporations is based.[29] Even *Business Week*, in an article that was generally laudatory of the agricultural corporations for launching a new "green revolution," noted that "regulators and food-policy officials already are drawing an analogy between Microsoft Corp.'s dominance in software operating systems and the life-sciences companies' control of seed technology."[30]

Perhaps the most controversial area of bio-engineering is the development of what are called "terminator seeds." To protect their patents and prevent farmers from replanting the bio-engineered seeds, genetic material is spliced into the new plants so that their seeds are rendered sterile. It is even conceivable that some characteristics of these terminator seeds could affect traditional crops. According to Pat Mooney of the Rural Advancement Foundation of Canada, "these technologies are extremely dangerous because over 1.4 billion farmers—primarily poor farmers in Africa, Asia and Latin America—depend on farm-saved seed as their primary seed source. If they can't save seed, they can't continue to adapt crops to their unique farming environments, and that spells disaster for global food security."[31]

THE MEDIA CONGLOMERATES

While corporate bio-engineering affects our life processes, the media corporations are unceasingly involved in shaping and intruding into our daily lives. The sway of these corporations has expanded enormously with the technologies of the information age. In the age of the robber barons, the media meant only the newspapers. Some of the great magnates of the period, like James Hill, bought newspapers to advance their political and economic interests while a few, like William Randolph Hearst and Horace Greely, became newspaper tycoons.[32]

In the early twentieth century, the media came to include the radio and the cinema, and then in the 1950s, television and the TV Networks. In the last 15 to 20 years, the size and scope of the major media corporate holdings have exploded to include Intranet, satellite and cable TV as well as newspapers, book and magazine publishing, Hollywood studios, and TV and radio networks. Ben H. Bagdikian first captured the emerging power of these businesses in *The Media Monopoly*, released in 1983. By 1997, in the preface to the fifth edition, Bagdikian was describing a very different world as he wrote:

> Nothing in earlier history matches this corporate group's power to penetrate the social landscape ... this handful of giants has created what is, in effect, a new communications cartel ... Aided by the digital revolution and the acquisition of subsidiaries that operate at every step in the mass communications process, from the creation of content to its delivery into the home, the communications cartel has exercised stunning influence...[33]

Today there are five major media empires: AOL-Time Warner, the largest in the world, which had merged with Turner Broadcasting in 1996, a media giant in its own right; Bertelsmann, a large German multimedia conglomerate with extensive interests in the United States as well as Europe; the well-known Disney media empire that also includes ABC; News Corporation, the media giant that owns Fox Network and is controlled by the arch-reactionary Rupert Murdoch; and Viacom-CBS, headed by Sumner Redstone and Mel Karmazin. The next tier of media companies includes PolyGram, a Dutch firm formerly owned by Philips, which is prominent in the recording industry; Seagram of Canada, which owns Universal Studios; Sony, the Japanese electronics firm that is active in music and TV; and General Electric, which owns NBC.[34]

If there is an "evil media empire," it is Rupert Murdoch's News Corporation. Even his fellow media moguls mince no words in describing him. Sumner Redstone says "he basically wants to conquer the world" while Ted Turner, now of Time Warner, likens Murdoch to Hitler.[35] Bill Gates, in an interview with the BBC in January 2000, suggested that Murdoch has too much influence in the media. In his takeover of major newspapers, particularly in

England and the United States, Murdoch has stomped on newspaper trade unions and imposed a "yellow journalism" which rivals that of late nineteenth-century media tycoons like William Randolph Hearst. Seeking to expand his sports fiefdom beyond the extensive sports programming carried on the Fox network, Murdoch has bought up the Los Angeles Dodgers, one of the oldest family-owned franchises in baseball history. He also established his own Australian rugby league with rules that condone more player viciousness and violence than the established Australian National Rugby League, whose owners had earlier rejected Murdoch's attempts to buy into their league.

Personalities aside, the media conglomerates serve as the primary boosters of globalization in the information age, shaping cultures and societies in the name of market capitalism. As Edward Herman and Robert McChesney write: "The global media are the missionaries of our age, promoting the virtues of commercialism and the market loudly and incessantly through their profit-driven and advertising-supported enterprises and programming."[36] Moreover, the media, while it lauds the "freedom" of the market place, has a distinctly anti-democratic edge. As the media monopolies spread their tentacles into virtually every facet of our existence, never have so few had so much power to shape the lives of so many.

In the United States media companies are monopolistic in many markets. Ninety-nine per cent of the 1,500 newspapers in the country are the only daily in their cities, while of the approximately 12,000 cable systems, all but a handful are monopolies in their markets.[37] The strong influence of the media conglomerates over U.S. government policy was demonstrated with the passage of the Telecommunications Act in 1996. The bill eliminated many of the consumer and diversity in programming protections contained in the original 1934 Act. Spending "forty million dollars' worth of lobbying" according to the *New York Times*, the bill allows companies to buy up multiple radio and TV stations in the same market and led to the acquisition or mergers of a number of media companies across the United States.[38]

THE HIGH-TECH BANKING INDUSTRY

In both the late nineteenth century and the information age, bankers and financiers have played a key role in underwriting and consolidating the new corporate order. At the turn of the twentieth century J.P. Morgan stood at the apex of the U.S. banking system, operating as the country's virtual chair of banking in an era when there was no Federal Reserve system. According to Josephson, in the 1890s Morgan used his financial power "to eliminate competition from the railroad business," while forging industrial trusts such as the International Harvester Company and the General Electric Company.[39] Perhaps his greatest business coup was the founding of the U.S. Steel Corporation with the purchase of Carnegie's steel interests and the takeover of many smaller steel companies.

Today, at the end of the twentieth century, there is as yet no single bank comparable to the House of Morgan. But the banking and financial firms are consolidating at a rapid pace and the U.S. may soon see a trillion dollar bank in terms of assets. In 1998, there were three major bank consolidations: Citigroup, a merger of Citibank and Travelers Groups with combined assets of almost $700 billion; BankAmerica, which subsumed Nationsbank under its name, with assets totaling $570 billion; and Banc One, which took over First Chicago, creating a $240 billion giant.[40] *Business Week* predicted that the main beneficiaries "will be companies, and families that have complex finances," meaning that the banks will lose interest in the small guy, or the "plain-vanilla checking accounts."[41] These megabanks are using the technologies of the information age to extend their influence and financial control to every corner of the planet. Susan Strange, the author of the path-breaking book *Casino Economy*, which captured the financial get-rich philosophy of the Reagan and Thatcher years in the banking industry, proclaims in her latest study, *Mad Money*, that the new technologies of the banking and finance systems have "changed the prevailing system ... out of all recognition."[42] The top banks are now global financial power-houses that include commercial and investment banking, and an array of financial services, ranging from insurance and credit cards to stock brokerage and mutual funds.

Business Week, in its special report on "The 21st Century Economy," declared that there has been a "financial revolution in the past 25 years," and that "financial technology will keep feeding off information technology." These changes favor further consol-idation of the banking industry, with one financial analyst predicting that in the next eight years "financial services will be dominated by five to ten global companies."[43] The new BankAmerica chairman, Hugh McColl, notes that the Internet alone enables the banking industry to achieve global economies of scale. "Technology has certainly improved American productivity in general and it's certainly improved productivity here [in banking]," declares McColl.[44]

As the subtitle of Strange's new book indicates, "When Markets Outgrow Governments," she is also concerned with how the technologies of the information age have enabled financial institutions to escape from regulatory controls, particularly in international markets. The trading of derivatives—which is essentially betting on the future of commodity prices, interest rates and especially currency exchange rates—is an untaxed and unregulated area of speculation that has boomed in recent years, with annual growth rates as high as 40 per cent. According to the IMF, derivative contracts in 26 countries in March 1995 totaled $47.5 trillion dollars, twice the value of world economic output.[45] It was in part the speculation on currencies through hedging and derivative contracts that brought down the Asian economies in 1997, and then led Long Term Capital Management, a U.S. fund that specialized in derivatives, to temporarily close its doors until it was bailed out in a deal backed by the U.S. Federal Reserve.

Money laundering and organized crime have also boomed with global banking. As Strange declares, "it would have hardly been possible to design a 'non-regime' that was better suited than the global banking system to the needs of drug dealers and other illicit traders who want to conceal from the police the origin of their large illegal profits."[46] Citibank, the major banking predecessor of Citigroup, has been deeply involved in some of the biggest money laundering scandals. In Mexico, Citibank was the "bank of choice" for Raul Salinas de Gortari, the brother of the former Mexican president, who is now in prison. Most of some $95 million in payoffs from drug traffickers to Salinas have been located in Swiss bank accounts that were handled by Citigroup. And in Pakistan, Citibank is charged with transferring some $40 million in bribes and kickbacks abroad on behalf of former Pakistani Prime Minister Benazir Bhutto, and her husband, Asiff Zardari.[47] In late 1999 the biggest money laundering scandal of all broke when it was revealed that the Bank of New York had laundered hundreds of millions of dollars on behalf of Russian mafia and governmental figures.

THE POLITICAL OPERATIVES OF THE INFORMATION AGE

In describing the power of the robber barons in the late nineteenth century, Matthew Josephson wrote: "political institutions [were] conquered, its social philosophy turned into a pecuniary one."[48] He wrote that "the railroad presidents, the copper barons, the big dry-good merchants and the steel masters became Senators, ruling in the highest councils of the national government," passing legislation and shaping economic policies that favored their interests.[49]

Today, the entrepreneurs of the information age are not as interested in directly occupying the seats of political power, but the entire class of high-tech robber barons, especially the media moguls and the bankers, is increasingly intent on exercising its sway over governments. This is in large part why Citibank is so anxious to assist the likes of Salinas and Bhutto in the world. The new barons curry favor with government leaders in order to expand their power and influence along with the bottom line of their financial reports.

In the United States in 1998 and 1999, when Congress was largely gridlocked due to the Monica Lewinsky affair, the war in the Balkans and partisan conflict between Republicans and Democrats, the high-tech business sector was able to exert widening clout in Washington D.C. and move its legislative agenda forward. Headed by a new lobbying group, the Information Technology Industry Council, high-tech firms more than doubled their political donations to candidates between 1996 and 1998. High tech companies now stand among the top donors of soft money to the Republican and Democratic parties. And the donations have paid off. By late 1999, the high-tech sector had gotten legislation exempting all Internet commerce from taxes, an extension of tax credits for research and development, special visas for skilled foreign workers that undermined the salaries of U.S. technical workers, legislation exempting companies from any lawsuits stemming from the Year 2000 computer glitch, and a relaxation of curbs on high-tech exports.[50]

With the indictment of Microsoft for monopolistic practices by the Democratic administration, Bill Gates and Microsoft have significantly stepped up their political donations to the Republican Party. Microsoft and its executives ranked 11th on the list of soft money donors to the GOP, giving almost $600,000 in 1997–98.[51] The Democrats received one-quarter of that amount, a reversal of past political funding patterns, such as the 1992 elections when the Republicans got only 20 per cent of Microsoft's total donations. Of

Microsoft's seven lobbyists in Washington, one is ex-chief of staff to House Majority Leader Dick Armey (Republican, Texas), and another is an ex-GOP Senate staffer.[52] One Microsoft executive asserts the company is "steadfastly bipartisan, while Microsoft spokesman Greg Shaw declares the company is only "sharing its views and experience" with political leaders.[53]

The efforts of these corporations to influence and manipulate government policies are only in their early stages. As the different sectors of the high-tech world consolidate, so will their influence and links to the government. Already, as we have seen in one of the most advanced sectors—media and telecommunications—these companies lobbied intensely to pass the Telecommunications Act of 1996, which sacrificed public interests and needs for those of the private sector.

As Todd Gitlin, a noted student of the media and the high-tech age, declares:

> Trusts with an immense capacity for overbearing power are being merged and acquired into existence as if there were nothing at stake but stock values. Today's deals may weigh on the culture for decades ... If the country believed in the countervailing authority of the government, the recourse would be obvious: Time for the sheriff to step in ... But the sheriff has been disarmed—at least politically. It suits the parties in power to collect impressive sums from the titans while proclaiming the virtues of self-regulation. If the issue were street crime, conservatives would be crying out against such an abject surrender.[54]

The original robber barons were brought to heel to a limited extent by the enforcement of anti-trust legislation in the early twentieth century. However, the power and wealth of their corporations and families remained enormous and helped propel the stock market boom of the 1920s that benefited the few at the top—like the Morgans and the Rockefellers—while farmers and workers languished at the bottom with stagnant or declining wages and incomes. The collapse of the stock market and the Great Depression of the 1930s led to the first real checks on the political and economic power of the robber barons and their successors, with the passage of the New Deal legislation under Franklin Delano Roosevelt.

It is notable that much of this earlier legislation regulating business, such as the Glass-Steagall Banking Act of 1933 and the

Communications Act of 1934, has been eroded or repealed under pressure from today's corporate and financial elites. As regards anti-trust legislation, excepting a few token prosecutions like that of Microsoft, there is no need for repeal since U.S. executives from Ronald Reagan onward have given the green light to the wave of corporate mergers that have taken place in the so-called new economy. Just as occurred in the early twentieth century, we are witnessing an economic boom driven largely by the stock market while the income of those at the bottom languishes. Only time will tell if the world has to suffer another collapse of the financial markets and a global depression in order to bring an end to the unquenchable greed and perniciousness of the new robber barons.

Part Two

Politics in a Postmodern Age

4   Shades of Postmodern Politics

A postmodern political age has emerged along with the epoch of globalization. It is difficult to articulate a nexus between the two, as the changes taking place in the political realm are far more complex and tangled than the transformations associated with the process of globalization. Some of the critical political shifts of recent decades can be readily discerned: the collapse of communism and most of the political parties on the left, the related decline in importance of political ideologies, the rise of protest movements centered around issues of identity, race, gender and religion, the hollowness of traditional political parties as they become instruments run and controlled by elites, and the growing alienation of the public in general from political parties as politics is reduced to media campaigns and political spectacles.

To understand the age of postmodern politics, an attempt must first be made to comprehend the elusive idea of postmodernity. Postmodernity is commonly viewed as a condition, largely cultural, that penetrates many aspects of contemporary life. It is closely linked to mass consumerism, the rise of the information and the media ages, the constant sense of change and impermanence, and in its extreme form, the breakdown of the barriers between reality, fiction, appearance and imagination. This is an age of malaise and uncertainty, a period in which the values of rationality and positivism that date from the Enlightenment are challenged as relativistic perspectives hold increasing sway.

Postmodern politics also eludes easy definition. No one goes around campaigning for postmodern politics or declaring they are postmodern politicians. On the most superficial level, postmodern politics involves the use and manipulation of the media. In this limited sense there are many politicians of varying political stripes who are de facto practitioners of postmodern politics. Bill Clinton, for example, is a postmodern politician. So also was Ronald Reagan, the "Teflon President," and John F. Kennedy, the first world leader to use the TV so effectively as to breach the boundary between real achievements and illusional accomplishments with the imagery of the New Frontier and Camelot. What makes all three of them politicians with a postmodern edge is their facility to manipulate the media and to create images, to put a political spin on developments and to generate political spectacles that often blur the line between hype and reality.

Lyndon Johnson and Richard Nixon were the antithesis of postmodern politicians. Both failed abysmally in their use of the media. Johnson, with his back-room deals, his arm-twisting and his power brokering represented the culmination of the old style politics that did not play well with the public media. Nixon was brought down not simply by the Watergate break-in and his paranoid style of politics, but also by his inability to master and project on the TV screen. This was the politician with the perpetual five o'clock shadow who had an uptight demeanor when talking to reporters or appearing on television. His antipathy towards the media was expressed most openly in 1962 when, after losing the governor's race in California, he told the press "you won't have Richard Nixon to kick around anymore." All these limits help explain why Watergate became a political spectacle that Nixon could not control.

The Clinton presidency provides us with an especially interesting case study of politics in the postmodern age. Clinton and his advisers may have won the 1992 campaign with the refrain "It's the economy, stupid." But what they learned once in power is "It's the spectacle, stupid." Clinton held firmly onto the presidential office in the midst of an unprecedented assault from the right, not because of a simplistic focus on the economy but because he mastered the politics of the spectacle. It is little short of astounding that, right after Clinton was impeached because of the Lewinsky affair, his popularity ratings jumped to the highest level of his presidency. The key to his survival was his mastery of the correct political spin, or "image projection" throughout the scandal. While proclaiming that he would not let impeachment distract him from "carrying out the people's business," he expressed public contrition in soap opera style for having "an improper relationship."

The Republicans became the straight, "modern" politicians who sought to skewer Clinton on sex and morality issues, ignoring the relativistic approach of a postmodern age that is largely unconcerned with traditional morality and a strict interpretation of legalities. If anything, Clinton's sexual peccadilloes captured the U.S. popular imagination. And exposés of the extramarital relationships of Republican congressmen by Larry Flint and Salon on the Internet only contributed to the multimedia melodrama, as Henry Hyde and Robert Livingston became the "outed" hypocrites clamoring against Clinton.

These interpretations of U.S. presidential politics from a postmodern perspective are only surface manifestations of profound changes in the technological and social arenas that have altered the realm of politics. Underlying the new age of postmodern politics is, first and foremost, the transformation of telecommunications and the mass media. Three key innovations have made this possible: the development of the television, particularly color TV, as a mass phenomenon; the placing of synchronous satellites in orbit that instantly transmit media signals around the world; and, finally, the rise of the Internet and the personal computer, which make it possible to send and access information around the globe at any particular moment. These core innovations and their many accessories—cellular phones, modems, VCRs, etc.—have linked the world together and created an international media culture that profoundly affects politics.

IDEOLOGY AND POSTMODERN POLITICS

Complementing these technological transformations in the age of postmodern politics is the decline of ideology. It is not simply that the public is increasingly unconcerned with ideology as mass consumerism and the fetishism of the market place penetrate every corner of the globe. More fundamentally, the three main political ideologies that have driven the Western world since the French revolution—liberalism, conservatism and then socialism—are in disarray or no longer functional. They are unable to explain or incorporate the tremendous complexity and diverse realities of the contemporary world. Francis Fukuyama has argued that this is the end of history because of the triumph of liberal democratic capitalism over communism.[1] He is right that we have reached an end, but it is not the Hegelian end in the sense of the permanent triumph of a particular system. Rather, it is the culmination or climax of a long legacy of Western political philosophies as modern political systems fail us in every major region of the world.

In Africa political modernization is in a profound crisis—neither the single party states, nor the liberal free market governments supported by the West are working. In Asia the strong centralized authoritarian regimes as well as the formal democracies are also in a state of crisis to one degree or another, as revealed by events in Indonesia, Malaysia, China and both Koreas. And in Latin America the dictatorships of the 1970s and 1980s have been superseded by formal democracies but they are not authentic participatory democracies that respond to fundamental needs. Today Latin America has the greatest disparities in income between the rich and the poor of any region in the world, reflecting the inability of their political systems to deal with serious economic distortions and injustices.[2]

In the sites of the oldest democracies, the United States and western Europe, democracy is becoming highly formalized with politically alienated populaces and increasing voter apathy. Political parties are no longer organs of mass participation but instead media driven bureaucracies that function on behalf of the politicians and the vested interests who control them. In the United States in particular, the two main parties have become huge fund-raising organizations beholden to corporate and big moneyed interests as they strive to raise the enormous budgets necessary to pay pollsters, media consultants, and of course the news and media networks that are contracted to broadcast their political messages.

Running parallel to the decline of ideology and mass-based political parties is the social fragmentation of postmodern societies. We are in the period of late capitalism, when industrial Fordism based on mass production has been overshadowed by the rise of flexible accumulation, a system in which corporations are constantly searching for and moving to cheaper labor pools while producing for specialty and niche markets. With flexible accumulation, the financial, advertising and service sectors of the economy increase in importance while the turnover time necessary to shift from one product to another is substantially reduced.

This economic shift has undermined traditional class society and generates entirely new social strata with distinct political and cultural interests. As Perry Anderson writes in *The Origins of Postmodernity*:

> Late capitalism remained a class society, but no class within it was quite the same as before. The immediate vector of postmodern culture was certainly to be found in the stratum of newly affluent employees and professionals created by the rapid growth of the

service and speculative sectors of the developed capitalist societies. Above this brittle yuppie layer loomed the massive structures of the multinational corporations themselves—vast servo-mechanisms of production and power, whose operations criss-cross the global economy, and determine its representations in the collective imaginary. Below, as an older industrial order is churned up, traditional class formations have weakened, while segmented identities and localized groups, typically based on ethnic or sexual differences, multiply.[3]

Partially as a result of these socio-economic shifts, we are witnessing political fragmentation and the rise of single-issue politics that appeal to the new social strata.[4] The old class politics based on trade unions and a numerous industrial working class is waning in importance. In the United States in 1998, when unemployment dipped to the lowest level in 28 years, every major category of employment increased except for manufacturing, which declined in absolute and relative numbers. This helps explain why political ori-entations are now relatively less determined by clear-cut class issues and more so by social and cultural cleavages rooted in gender, race and ethnic divisions, as well as by one's location on the educa-tional/social ladder of the information age.

ALL THAT'S LEFT

The traditional left has virtually disappeared due to the changes of the postmodern age. For the communist parties in the Western world, the decline of the blue-collar working class has effectively destroyed their *raison d'être*. And in the communist societies of eastern Europe, much is made of the failure of their economic system to compete with capitalism. While this was a factor, it is perhaps more important to understand the changes wrought in the social structure of the communist societies. As the command socialist economies grew in complexity over the decades, so did the intricacy of their societies. The growing intelligentsia and middle classes yearned for change, aspiring not solely to the consumer goods of the Western world, but also to the new social and cultural attributes that they were increasingly exposed to via the globalized media. Originally rooted in the ideals of the "New Man," by the 1980s the communist parties had become brittle and unresponsive bureaucracies, often able in fact to deliver the "bread and butter," but increasingly devoid of any real ideals or creativity that responded to the new interests and conditions of the postmodern age.

Given the demise of socialism and communist societies, can it be said that the postmodern condition has mainly reinforced and advanced the interests of neo-liberalism and capitalist consumer societies in general, as some on the left have suggested? While it is often overlooked, it is important to recognize that a new progressive, even radical, orientation compatible with the changes of the postmodern age began to emerge in the social and political upheavals of the 1960s. The civil rights and anti-war movements were the central struggles of the early and mid-1960s, particularly in the United States, but they quickly expanded into different arenas, including a strong counter-cultural current that broke with established values. These movements reached their global apogee in 1968 with the Paris uprising, the Prague Spring, the riots at the Democratic Convention in Chicago, and the student uprising in Mexico City. None of these struggles achieved political power, but they changed the world. The new social movements and the cultural values they reflected could not be contained as they undermined the established political systems as well as conventional social values and regressive relations that existed between races, sexes, communities, nations and even individuals.

In the decades since then, many diverse currents of thinking have emerged within the left. To understand this diversity and fragmentation of thought, it is necessary to move beyond the condition of postmodernity and postmodern politics to embark on a discussion of the philosophy of postmodernism. Many argue that postmodern philosophy, with its negation of absolutes, its discarding of metanarratives, and its reveling in the politics of the spectacle, directly undermines progressive political and social struggles. While there certainly are adverse reverberations of postmodern philosophy, a number of progressive and radical thinkers have turned to postmodern thought to develop a more effective critique of capitalist societies and of the political and cultural discourses that sustain the power of the dominant classes.

One progressive school of postmodernist orientation focuses on deconstructing postcolonial structures and the imperial domination of peoples in the third world. For example, *Cultures of United States Imperialism*, edited by Amy Kaplan and Donald Pease, critiques the dominant cultural attitudes and perspectives that have obscured U.S. intervention and exploitation of other parts of the world.[5] Another edited anthology, *Close Encounters of Empire*, reinterprets the use of images and historical texts in key episodes of U.S. intervention and domination in Latin America, including the U.S. war against Sandino in Nicaragua, the establishment of United Fruit enclaves in Colombia, and the U.S. occupation of the Dominican Republic and its backing of the Trujillo regime. The final chapter, by Maria del Carmen Suescum Pozas, "From Reading to Seeing: Doing and Undoing Imperialism in the Visual Arts," uses eleven groups of images to raise a series of questions and issues about how we can debunk the concepts of domination and replace them with new images and narratives that reflect the lives of those who suffer from exploitation and political repression.[6]

Other works have taken a close look at some of the original theorists of postmodernism to try to understand what can or cannot be useful for the development of a new radical politics. Honi Fern Haber in *Beyond Postmodern Politics* scrutinizes the thought of Jean-Francois Lyotard, Richard Rorty and Michel Foucault. She concludes that postmodern thought can be liberating, that "it lays bare the artifice of all grand narratives and so frees us to create our individual and collective lives, to articulate our own voices."[7] But Haber goes on to point out that some postmodern theorists maintain that all political structures are exploitative, thereby making it difficult to come up with a political theory that legitimizes collective action and oppositional politics.

Haber also asserts that postmodernists lose "the political game" if they engage in random, disconnected discourses. Such an extreme focus on differences, "far from giving voice to the marginalized Other, deprives that Other of any meaningful language."[8] She goes on to insist that an effective oppositional politics first needs "to encourage self-respect and self-knowledge among individuals whose identity has either been silenced, devalued, or erased," and that once this is accomplished, these individuals can work in various communities to disrupt and challenge the existing, oppressive social and political structures.[9]

Cultural Politics by Glenn Jordan and Chris Weedon is a path-breaking study of how culture in the postmodern age has become integral to our political life. The authors draw on postmodernist thinking on language, subjectivity and power to look at the cultural politics of class, gender and race. In these three social arenas, they conclude: "Cultural politics involve a struggle over meaning ... Meaning is both a channel for power and its legitimation. Culture politics is also a struggle for subjectivities. Through culture, identities and subjectivities are produced."[10]

Jordan's and Weedon's case studies lead them to concur with the postmodernist tenet that there is no singular truth. "Truths are discursive constructs which differ across histories and cultures, as well as between different interest groups within the same culture. Whoever has the power to define Truth in any society also has the power to define Others."[11]

However, like Heber, Jordan and Weedon also see dangers for political action in a postmodern theory that argues against any universals or even partial metanarratives. They believe that some universals, like universal human rights, for example, may be relative and historically determined, but they are necessary, even essential, for the struggle of women, peoples of color, and the oppressed in general. In their concluding paragraph, they point to the downside of postmodernists who celebrate plurality and pleasure while ignoring power and the need for effective resistance:

> Where postmodern difference is seen as pluralism without attention to the social location of difference, power and its effects become invisible. Here difference often appears as a form of radical chic, indifferent to the (often brutal) power relations that structure difference. The postmodern move from History to histories can be productive and empowering for groups usually absent from History. But here, too, not all histories are equal. To ignore power, for example by treating all histories as if they had equal status and power, leads to a denial of specificity of oppressions.[12]

One can conclude from the above authors that postmodern thought as it relates to politics is an intellectual minefield. There is much in it that can be useful for our critique of the dominant order, but it can also lead to complete relativism, nihilism and a belief that political and social struggles are meaningless. But, for better or worse, the left needs to enter into this debate and discussion. This is a postmodern age, not simply because of the existence of postmodern theory, but because the world itself has changed dramatically in recent decades. Culture, the mass media, the fragmentation of classes, flexible accumulation, the growth of consumerism, and the prominence of the spectacle all make it imperative that we develop new perspectives and approaches for understanding and involving ourselves in the postmodern age.

POSTMODERN LEFT VS. POSTMODERN RIGHT

A slender volume by Hans-Georg Betz, *Postmodern Politics in Germany*, points the way to how we can decipher politics and societies in the postmodern age. Betz argues that in Germany the postmodern condition in politics is manifested in the rise of two alternative political formations, the Greens on the left, and the Republikaner party on the right. The Greens emerged in Germany in the mid-1970s when many began to question traditional political approaches and advocated new values that emphasized environmental, cultural and identity issues.

In the 1980s, however, the new right gained momentum in opposition to the established political order and also as a reaction to the cultural and political values advocated by groups and organizations like the Greens. As Betz notes, the Greens and the new right

> represent two diametrically opposed facets of a new politics ... Grounded less in the representation of interests than in the representation of a variety of new values, they articulate broadly what are rapidly becoming two of the most important emerging cultural priorities of Western Europe's post industrial societies: on one hand the preservation of the natural environment, on the other the protection of national and cultural identity.[13]

Writing in 1991, Betz was on the cusp of the collapse of East Germany and the emergence of a reunited Germany. Developments since then, such as the rebirth of the old east Germany communist party as the Party of Democracy, and the growth of a radical right-wing xenophobic youth movement in the former east Germany, only reinforce Betz's contention that the postmodern age is an ongoing process "of social fragmentation and individualization, political dealignment and realignment."[14]

The rise to power in 1998 of the SPD with a new junior partner, the Greens, may not have led to any basic transformations of the political system, but it reflects the altered political debates and the volatility of politics in Germany and Europe at large. The elections in Hesse in February 1999, coming just a hundred days after the SPD-

Green coalition took power, revealed that struggles over ethnic and environmental politics remain at the heart of politics. By attacking the new government's proposed legislation to liberalize German citizenship requirements and its efforts to abandon nuclear plants, the Christian Democrats took control of the Hesse state government and accentuated tensions between the SPD and the Greens.

Some of the theorists of the new right in Germany and Europe draw explicitly on postmodernist thought to argue for the enforcement of traditional moral values, the re-establishment of strict law and order to combat crime and drugs, and the expulsion of third world immigrants and foreign workers. Two such theorists, Armin Mohler and Pierre Krebs of Germany, reject universalist ideologies, particularly that of modernist, liberal societies that uphold egalitarianism. They argue that these universals condone the destruction of diversity, originality and particularity. These values can only be preserved in the hierarchically structured whole of a group or nation with a similar cultural heritage. Krebs asserts that the new right in Europe needs to strengthen "the Europeans in their particularity and difference" while encouraging "other races to preserve their particularity" by not mingling with the Europeans."[15]

Alone with these rightist, postmodern philosophical currents, the broader right-wing ethnic chauvinist movements of Europe feed off the crises of the modernist political systems, be they of the communist or liberal variants. The collapse of the communist political order in eastern Europe, particularly in Yugoslavia, opened up the old ethnic antagonisms that the communist leaders had never dealt with, except through repression or the formal establishment of constitutions and laws that decreed on paper that all races and nationalities are equal. And in western Europe in the 1990s the swelling of the ranks of the unemployed with late capitalism and the rise of flexible accumulation have abetted the new right's campaigns for the exclusion of foreign workers and immigrants across the continent.

The complexities of the struggles in Europe and elsewhere make it difficult to try to use any single overview or totalizing philosophy to explain what is happening. As the past history of Europe in particular demonstrates, idealistic and utopian metanarratives, including messianic religions, Nazism, and even communism, have resulted in the loss of millions of lives as one group or another sought to impose its beliefs and values on others. Karl Marx, the leading theorist of socialism and communism, projected an extremely humane and democratic future for socialist societies, but his totalizing philosophy was all too easily distorted by leaders who repressed and even murdered in the name of imposing their vision on the countries they ruled.

However, the abandonment of utopian metanarratives by many on the left does not mean that the struggles for social justice, democracy and economic equality are to be abandoned. Indeed, the collapse of communism, and even the deep-rooted skepticism about socialism as an alternative to capitalism, have not led to an abatement of progressive social and political struggles around the world. The challenges to established and repressive authorities are far too extensive to be listed here, but wherever one looks—in Europe, Asia, Latin America, the United States etc.—social explosions continue to occur and critical battles are being fought, and even won by progressive social forces.

Virtually every year since the breakup of the Soviet Union in 1991 has witnessed a critical social revolt or uprising. In 1992, south central Los Angeles erupted in violence in the aftermath of the acquittal of police officers who had savagely beaten Rodney King. On January 1, 1994, the Zapatista uprising occurred in Mexico, and later in the year Nelson Mandela and the African National Congress took power in South Africa. In the mid-1990s mass protests by French workers and farmers brought their government's neo-liberal policies to a standstill. In 1997, Mobutu after a tyrannical reign in Zaire of over 30 years, was overthrown, and then in 1998, Suharto was tossed out as the ruler of Indonesia. The arrest of the Chilean dictator Augusto Pinochet in London in late 1998, while primarily the result of advances in the international legal system, reflected years of patient grassroots work by human rights and solidarity organizations. And, as the century ended, the East Timorese won their freedom from the brutal rule of the Indonesian military. Finally, the battle in Seattle over the expansion of the World Trade Organization revealed that the opposition to globalization was becoming globalized as people from all over the world assembled in Seattle. While the left has not seized state power as a result of any of these upheavals, with the singular exception of South Africa, some of the more odious forms of state rule and repression have been challenged and even ended. Given the altered power of the state apparatus in the epoch of globalization, it may be more effective in many instances to wage an ongoing struggle for change from below rather than holding formal power.

In the United States, the conventional wisdom is that the conservative right wing is now in the ascendancy, that it has eclipsed progressives and is even able to challenge a Democratic president whose views and policies often have more in common with Republicans than liberal Democrats. But it should be remembered that, like the right wing in Europe, U.S. conservatives are in large part reacting to the many progressive advances that have been made in the decades since the upheaval of the 1960s. The so-called cultural wars, particularly over education, are in large part an attempt by the right to reverse past advances, and it is by no means clear that conservatives are winning these wars. Paul Weyrich, an ideologue and strategist of the new right, was so dismayed in early 1999 by setbacks in the culture wars that he acknowledged there is no "moral majority" and urged conservatives to "drop out" and "quarantine" themselves from the rest of society.[16]

There is no singular analysis or vision that will propel the left forward. This is an age where we have to be open to a large number of perspectives and viewpoints. Ariel Salleh, in *Ecofeminism as Politics: Nature, Marx and the Postmodern*, makes a strong argument for drawing on a number of approaches to help shape a new politics. Ecofeminist politics, she declares, is "an uncompromising critique of capitalist patriarchal culture;" it is socialist because it sides with "the wretched of the earth;" it is an ecology "because it reintegrates humanity with nature;" and it is a postmodern and postcolonial discourse "because it focuses on deconstructing Eurocentric domination."[17]

In the postmodern age, "All That's Left" is a largely undefined left undergoing an enormous transition as it tries to endure. Since the 1960s the left has in a certain sense gone underground, resurfacing almost invisibly in the feminist and social movements, the civil rights movement, the gay rights movements, the environmental movement, and in recent years, once again in the workers movement. All these movements are basically internationalist in their linkages and perspectives, thereby helping to sustain a broader global orientation. We may no longer rely on metanarratives or utopian ideals, but perhaps it is better that way. The technological, cultural and ideological transformations of the postmodern age now make it possible to have very concrete tasks and particular visions of what we are about and what we can do to help make a better world.

The technologies of the information age are of course primarily used and manipulated by corporate interests. But this should not blind us to the reality that these technologies can be used to promote social justice and democratic interests. Perhaps the most renowned illustration of the employment of such technologies for radical democratic causes is the Zapatista movement's use of the Internet to announce its insurrection. As the last chapter points out, subsequent communiqués were relayed over the Internet, and several years later the Internet played a critical role in organizing and publicizing the Intergalactic international gathering in the rain forests of Chiapas.

Democratic struggles around the world now make use of the full range of communication devices, including personal computers, cellular phones, faxes, specially designed web pages, and chat rooms. The uprising against Suharto in Indonesia, the struggle for independence in East Timor, the ongoing battle for democracy in China, and the long fight of the Kurds in the Middle East for their own nation state—all these struggles, just as that of the Zapatistas, make use of the new technologies, particularly the Internet—to broadcast and propagate their struggles against repressive states and rulers.[18] Support and relief networks around human and natural tragedies, like Hurricane Mitch in Central America, are also rapidly put together using new communications technologies. Alternative strategies for rebuilding Central America, such as the detailed plan put out by over 300 NGOs in Nicaragua, were quickly communicated around the world using email and web sites.[19]

Obviously, the use of the technologies of the information age in no way guarantees the weakening or defeat of established positions of government and official institutions. But for the first time in history, the information age enables us to propagate and communicate our views to a broad international network almost instantaneously, even though corporate interests may own and dominate the new technologies. Future successes or failures in pursuing new options and alternatives will be determined by how effective popular and democratic movements are at using these new media to spread messages and ideas that mobilize people around their specific interests, needs and identities.

5   The (Un)defining of Postmodern Marxism

Marxism as a political ideology appears to have a dismal future as we begin the new century. The social forces that drove socialism for much of the last century—the working classes and the peasantry— show little interest in Marxism or socialist politics. Even the old communist and socialist parties in the Western and Eastern worlds that managed to survive the fall of the Berlin Wall and the collapse of the Soviet Union have largely abandoned Marxism as they try to adapt to the needs of the contemporary world. In China, communism's most important remaining enclave, Marxism-Leninism is used to justify the continued existence of a one party state as its leaders enrich themselves, often through corruption and the exploitation of the country's cheap labor force.

The collapse of Marxism has rendered the left and progressives largely powerless. If the left is to recapture the political high ground in the new century, a radical project needs to be rethought and rearticulated. As Russell Jacoby notes in *The End of Utopia*:

> Almost everywhere the left contracts, not simply politically but, perhaps more decisively, intellectually. To avoid contemplating the defeat and its implications, the left now largely speaks the language of liberalism—the idiom of pluralism and rights. At the same time, liberals, divested of a left wing, suffer from waning determination and imagination.[1]

To rebuild a philosophy of radical political thought, it no longer suffices to tinker with some of the premises of Marxism as was done by the broadly defined neo-Marxist school that arose in the aftermath of World War II and flourished in the 1960s and 70s. Today we need to go much further, particularly by exploring the major new arena of critical thinking referred to as postmodernism. On the surface, Marxism and postmodernism would appear to be at odds with each other, as some of the debates and clashes between the two illustrate.[2] But some have attempted to find a rapprochement between the two, to create what can be called a postmodern

Marxist position that combines what is useful in the classical and neo-Marxist traditions with critical perspectives and insights provided by postmodernism.

These efforts need to be distinguished from what is called "strong" postmodernism, best exemplified by Jacques Derrida. By insisting that all truth is relative and rejecting universalist constructs of any type, this school in effect undermines any political movements or ideas that are driven by basic social concerns.[3] Postmodern Marxism also needs to be separated from post-Marxist positions that have rejected virtually the entire Marxist tradition, holding that it is of little use in understanding the contemporary world. Here the work of Ernesto Laclau and Chantal Mouffe, as well as that of Michele Barrett embody this approach.[4]

In the intellectual and academic worlds, several currents of postmodern Marxist thought are emerging. One of the most prominent is what could be called the Amherst school, founded principally by Stephen Resnick and Richard Wolff.[5] Grouped around the journal, *Rethinking Marxism*, and the Association for Social and Economic Analysis (ASEA), the Amherst school draws heavily on the structuralist work of Louis Althusser, and is also influenced by Europeans such as Antonio Negri of Italy and Etienne Balibar of France.[6]

Characterizing its approach as anti-essentialist, this school argues that classical Marxism was methodologically too focused on drawing out the narrow, essentialist aspects of class, society and capitalism, thereby often leading Marxists into reductionist and/or functionalist approaches. The Amherst school asserts that, in order to understand the contemporary world, one needs to de-center Marxist analysis, to realize that there is no singular reality. Using this approach, J.K. Gibson-Graham, in *The End of Capitalism (As We Knew It)*, problematizes "capitalism as an economic and social descriptor." The book argues that, because "most economic discourse is 'capitalocentric,'... other forms of economy (not to mention noneconomic aspects of social life) are often understood primarily with reference to capitalism."[7] Gibson-Graham believes that the traditional Marxist view of capitalism as hegemonic and all encompassing actually weakens opposition to it and reinforces its ideological domination.

Another current of postmodern Marxism is represented by Frederic Jameson, Edward Soja and perhaps by David Harvey. They believe that capitalism has entered a new phase, a postmodern phase in which the Fordist system of capitalist production is replaced by flexible accumulation. Jameson, more than Harvey, has written extensively on postmodern culture. One difficulty with categorizing this current is that Harvey, while analyzing the nature of post-modernity, has refrained from describing himself as a postmodern Marxist. Jameson, however, has stated that "a postmodern capitalism necessarily calls a postmodern Marxism into existence over against itself," but none of his writings to date has described what consti-tutes postmodern Marxism.[8]

Edward Soja, a geographer like Harvey, goes much further in linking deconstruction to Marxism. He argues that four radical thinkers of the post-World War II era—Henri Lefebre, Ernest Mandel, Michel Foucault and John Berger—broke with the narrow historicism that had come to predominate much of Marxism as well as the estab-lished, highly compartmentalized, social sciences. According to Soja, these thinkers all understood to one degree or another that the dev-astating impact of imperialism and capitalism could be understood only by placing them in spatial, geographic contexts.[9]

New Left Review of London and its book-publishing arm, Verso Press, comprise an arena where discussions of postmodernism and its relationship to Marxism have flourished. Stuart Hall is perhaps the most prominent figure in this school, writing extensively on culture, society and politics, often breaking with more classical Marxist positions.[10] Verso Press also released a ground-breaking work in 1983, Marshall Berman's *All That Is Solid Melts Into Air*. Although Berman is opposed to hard postmodernism, he adopts a critique of modernity and an interpretation of Marx that draws on postmodern influences.[11]

In general, *New Left Review*, unlike *Monthly Review*, which has carried articles critical of postmodernism, is notable for its willing-ness to encourage a dialogue and interchange between different currents of Marxism and postmodernism. [12] However no article or tome by *New Left Review* has articulated exactly what constitutes a postmodern Marxist position.

One of the reasons why postmodern Marxism, except perhaps for the Amherst anti-essentialist school, has been so hesitant to stake out a clearly defined position is because it is cognizant of the postmodern argument that our understanding is largely relative, and that we should refrain from creating new universalist paradigms. This is a period where we have to be exploratory and tentative. Or to put it another way, just as we have had a "thousand Marxisms" over the years, it will be encouraging to see a wide variety of postmodern approaches to Marxism appear.

Another reason for refraining from trying to delineate what constitutes postmodern Marxism is that such an endeavor may simply enwrap us more deeply in academic-like debates at a moment when we need to be more involved in the real world. As Michael Ryan noted already in 1982, "millions have been killed because they were Marxists; no one will be obliged to die because s/he is a deconstructionist."[13] The viability of postmodern Marxism will not be determined by its ability to clearly enunciate itself, but by its capacity to influence and interact with ongoing social struggles in the actually existing world.

In this spirit, the remainder of this chapter addresses several areas where classical Marxism and neo-Marxism are particularly vulnerable and where postmodernism can help foster a new approach. First, I will look at modernism and modernization, discussing how they have shaped socialist as well as capitalist development schemes in the last half century. Then the next part will be a discussion of the main actors for radical social change in the new century.

MODERNIZATION AND PROGRESS

If there is one approach that can draw postmodern Marxists together it is a critique of the particularly egregious tendencies of modernity and modernization located in capitalist and socialist societies alike. The history of capitalism is closely linked to modernity while the failed socialist project was also all about modernization. Capitalism in this century vied with the communist parties and the national liberation movements primarily over which system could best introduce or carry forward the project of modernization. It is in this competitive, rapid rush to modernization where socialism ultimately failed in its bid to "bury capitalism."

Inextricably linked to the concept of modernization is the idea of progress and the supposed inevitability of the socialist project. Karl Marx's works and the *Communist Manifesto* are steeped in the idea of progress as it developed in nineteenth-century Europe. The clear-cut stages of history, the belief that the proletariat would replace the bourgeoisie, the linear view of human development, and the conviction that there was no other alternative to these forces of history—these are some of the clearest influences of the idea of progress on the Marxist project that have continued well into this century. Here is where postmodernism, with its critique of modernity and the relationship of the idea of progress to the Enlightenment, can be of critical importance in formulating a new approach to Marxism.

Some neo-Marxists have mounted a defense of Marxism against challenges by postmodernism. One of its defenders, Ellen Meiksins Wood, insists on clinging to the mantle of modernism, asserting that "modernity has not much to do with capitalism," and that therefore Marxists do not need to be critical of modernity or the fountainhead of modernity, the Enlightenment.[14]

Meiksins Wood is doing little more than splitting historical hairs when she tries to extricate the Enlightenment and modernity from capitalism with her argument that "the ideology of the French bourgeoisie in the eighteenth century had not much to do with capitalism ..."[15] Certainly, the bourgeoisie did not emerge in any society, even in Great Britain, with a full-blown ideology based on its class and class interests. But the rise of capitalism is virtually indistinguishable from the emergence of modernity and the idea of progress. As Michael Watts notes in *Reworking Modernity*, we should not fall into "reductionism" by arguing that "modernization is synonymous with capitalist logic," but at the same time "it is also imperative that these sets of realities not be ripped asunder."[16]

Moreover, in her historical argument Meiksins Wood identifies most of the ideas of the Enlightenment almost exclusively with the French philosophers, when in fact Great Britain—the birthplace of manufacturing capitalism in the eighteenth century—developed its own variant of the Enlightenment and the idea of progress. As a study of this period concludes, "the blossoming and spread of the idea of progress in England and Scotland during the eighteenth century is of central importance to the overall history of that idea itself ... and even to the emergence of the modern world."[17] The point is not that we should condemn the entire Enlightenment, be it of French or British origins, but that we should recognize that many concepts of this period, particularly the idea of progress, need to be critiqued for the adverse impact they have had on the contemporary world in general and on Marxist theory in particular.[18]

More important than these historic arguments is the failure of many Marxists and neo-Marxists to recognize the heavy toll that modernism has taken on the third world, where modernization and development marked the discourse that the capitalist powers and the Soviet Union used to impose their models on the so-called underdeveloped world. As Arturo Escobar points out in his seminal work, *Encountering Development: The Making and Unmaking of the Third World*,

> the organizing premise was the belief in the role of modernization as the only force capable of destroying archaic superstitions and relations, at whatever social, cultural and political cost. Industrialization and urbanization were seen as the inevitable and necessarily progressive routes to modernization.[19]

As Escobar notes at the inception of his work, "instead of the kingdom of abundance promised by theorists and politicians in the 1950s, the discourse and strategy of development produced its opposite: massive underdevelopment and impoverishment, untold exploitation and oppression."[20]

Escobar's last phrases are directed primarily at the development model imposed by capitalism. But it is clear that socialism has pursued its own variant of modernization, one that has also had devastating consequences. As Ponna Wignaraja notes in the essay "Rethinking Development and Democracy," "though Marxist theory was a little more explicit [than neo-classical theory] about issues of social justice and equity, issues such as participation, culture, gender and equity, and ecology were central to neither paradigm."[21]

The major distortions of virtually all twentieth-century socialist countries—such as the systematic degradation of the environment, the creation of ugly, urban industrial centers, the abandonment of authentic democracy for a top-down command system designed to expedite economic growth at any cost, and, finally, in the artistic and cultural realms, the endorsement of "realist" art and aesthetic values that often denied or undermined creative individuality—all are inextricably linked to the single-minded quest for modernity and modernization. Many neo-Marxists would of course assert that they were and are opposed to these distortions of the former socialist societies. But, by not borrowing from postmodernist discourse and undertaking a basic critique of the modernization project that has been imbued in Marxism since its inception, they have remained stuck in the past, unable to help renovate socialism.

THE NEW SOCIAL ACTORS

This critique of Marxism and its relationship to modernism pales in the light of its second and most critical flaw in the twenty-first century—the demise of its principal social actor, the proletariat. Marx and Engels saw the working class as the singular agent capable of overthrowing the bourgeoisie and capitalism. Later, Lenin and Mao positioned the peasantry as central allies of the proletariat in the struggle to overthrow the established order. The problem is that changes in the nature of capitalism itself, particularly in the epoch of globalization, have not only led to the decline of the peasantry, but also reduced and substantially altered the role of the working class.

Here postmodern Marxism can make its most vital contribution by articulating and constructing a new social basis for radical change. Postmodernism argues that society and classes are fragmented—that workers, peasants, indigenous societies and other social groups have very specific identities, depending on their location, culture, history and other factors. What postmodern Marxism does is accept this fragmentation as a reality. It remains Marxist in a classical sense—it recognizes that capitalism has become a universal system—while at the same time it is postmodernist in that it believes a multiplicity of social groups and fragmented classes exist in the era of globalization that have little or no relationship to the universalized proletariat enunciated by Marx and Engels.

Postmodernism is well situated to provide insights into these new social actors due to its strong links to the social and identity movements, particularly the feminist movement. For the past 30 years or more the social movements have been a critical force for social change—the ethnic and civil rights movements, particularly among exploited races and indigenous groups, the feminist movement, the ecological movement, the gay and lesbian movements, to name a few. A much ignored grouping is the peace, human rights and solidarity movements, which have also grown in importance in recent years. They have helped to create a new globalist perspective, one that is very different from the globalization project foisted on us by big capital.

Of course, in recent decades academic Marxists as well as socialist movements have recognized the need for broad political alliances in the struggle against capitalism and oppression. They have incorporated feminist and environmental issues into their platforms and debates as well as an awareness of the importance of ethnicity. But this has not been sufficient to alter the thrust of the historic socialist project. A real rupture is needed with the idea of the working class as the principal, or only, force capable of overthrowing capitalism. A postmodern Marxist approach with its emphasis on social and identity movements is most capable of making this break.

In this context, trade unions and workers should be viewed essentially as a critical social movement rather than as the sole central protagonist capable of overthrowing late capitalism.[22] Certainly, no major alterations of the current order can occur without the participation of the working classes, but neither can fundamental change occur without the active participation of the civil rights and ethnic movements, the feminist movement, the environmental movement, the peace and anti-war movements, and others, depending on the configuration of any given society.

An enormous amount of research and discussion around the social movements has been generated in recent years, which could not possibly be reviewed here. There is tremendous diversity among these movements, as is illustrated by the differences in composition and objectives of these movements in Latin America, Africa, Asia and the core capitalist countries. In one chapter in the edited anthology, *The Making of Social Movements in Latin America*, the author notes:

> There is a wide spectrum of social movements. Many of them center on specific actors, others are self-referential or monadic; some are synchronic and latent, others of long duration; some are the product of the intensification of capitalism, others of exclusion; some are unprecedented, perhaps ambiguous, constantly changing with polivalent meanings. All of the movements, based on identities that are often changing, are internally complex and produced themselves within novel historical processes. In short, they represent new historical movements in the making.[23]

THE CASTAWAYS

It is important to realize that the complex social movements and the laboring classes are not the only basis for radical change. Here we have to look to the large and growing sector of humanity that has been variously called the underclass, the marginalized, or the castaways of the capitalist world. Doug Henwood, in "Post What?"

in the September 1996 issue of *Monthly Review* is wrong in his critique of postmodernism and specifically in his criticism of Jeremy Rifkin's book, *The End of Work*.[24] Rifkin and others point to the decline of the direct employment of workers in basic industries by corporations and big business. "Dead capital," or machines along with microchips, have assumed greater and greater importance in the era of automation and robotization. The dramatic rise of unemployment in western Europe in recent years is the most obvious manifestation of this tendency of capitalism. This in turn leads to a shocking expansion of the underclass, those who can find no regular employment and are marginalized.

While many of the manufacturing jobs are migrating to the third world, manufacturing employment in that part of the world will never absorb the numbers it once did in the Western economies. The International Labor Organization reports that 30 per cent of the world's workforce is currently unemployed or underemployed. Countries like the so-called "Asian Tigers" and Brazil and Mexico have developed significant industrial working classes with the growth of manufacturing, but they do not constitute a majority of the working-age population in the third world, or even within their own countries. This lack of industrial and formal, structured jobs explains why increasing numbers of people are forced to live on the margins as part of an informal economy.

Henwood is partially right when he argues that many workers become part-time, or contracted employees in this era of "flexible employment" and flexible accumulation. But this only underscores the difficulty of organizing people against capital in the workplace since there are fewer and fewer centralized work sites.

These two interacting tendencies of late capitalism—its flexibility and its marginalization of peoples, and even entire countries as is happening in Africa—compel us to reconceive who the antagonists of capitalism are and how they can be organized. Certainly trade unions will continue to be important, but it is just as important to develop viable strategies to organize the underclass and the marginalized, as well as to incorporate the social movements in the process of radical social change.

What is lacking is any sort of common consciousness among this diverse group of economic and social actors. But this is where radical postmodern Marxist thought, by articulating what is happening in the real world, can help narrate a new approach for social transformation that includes the social movements as well as the growing economic underclass that is marginalized by late capitalism.

Our main task is to describe the diverse new social actors for change and to postulate how they can interact and confront the dominant political and economic classes. In a certain sense, we are attempting to do for the epoch of globalization what Marx did for the era of manufacturing capitalism, namely, describing the political and social processes at work and presenting a coherent approach for change that intellectuals and social activists can use to mobilize and organize, to help galvanize those at the bottom to transform the world.

The very concept of postmodern Marxism is a temporal one. It will not become a banner that people fight and die for; rather postmodern Marxism is a conceptual framework for viewing the diverse and different struggles that are unfolding in the era of globalization. These movements, over a period of time, will have to frame and characterize their struggles from the ground up, creating local, regional and international ties to other struggles and movements. Only they have the capacity to create new narratives that are capable of challenging globalization and replacing the state socialism of the twentieth century with new emancipatory projects.

Note

This chapter is based in large part on an article I wrote for *Rethinking Marxism*, "The (Un)defining of Postmodern Marxism: On Narrating New Social and Economic Actors," Spring, 1998.

6 The Virtually Existing Global Revolution

In the epoch of globalization, a variety of alternative approaches and dissident movements are emerging around the world, comprising what can be called a virtually existing global revolution. The rigidity of formal political institutions and the blatant corporate bias of global rule-making institutions, such as the IMF, the World Bank and the WTO, have driven grassroots movements to improvise and create new alternatives from the bottom up. This is a revolution unlike any we knew in the century past. It is a revolution that is taking place here and now as we change our own values, ideas and lives while fighting against the institutions that dominate us.

Every revolution up until now has been a national revolution, aimed at seizing control of the state. Owing to events such as the Zapatista uprising and the Battle of Seattle, we can begin to envision a break with the classical Marxist position of seeing formal political revolutions as the principal or sole means of transforming societies.[1] The transition from global capitalism to democratized societies and economies will occur much as the transition from feudalism to capitalism occurred—it will be a gradual process in which radical actions and activities, economic as well as social and political, take hold in the midst of the global capitalist order.

ALTERNATIVE ECONOMIES

We can begin to understand the unfolding of this virtual revolution by looking at some of the struggles that relate to the economic arena. A new economic agenda, however incipient and unconsolidated, is taking shape among progressive circles that breaks not only with neo-liberalism, but also with the legacy of the old communist societies that tried to develop the economic order from the so-called "commanding heights of the state."

The *End of Capitalism (As We Knew It)* by J.K Gibson-Graham argues that many of the economic activities in the contemporary world cannot be considered capitalist and that the existence of these activities provides space for us to imagine an alternative world.[2] Taking this approach, one can perceive numerous economic endeavors that comprise an incipient foundation for alternative democratic economies.

Among them are:

1. Worker-run cooperatives that have a significant regional or provincial presence, particularly in parts of Italy, Spain, France and Belgium.

2. The ESOPs, or Employee Stock Ownership Plans, in which trade unions and workers hold large or controlling blocks of shares in a given company. There are 10,000 ESOPs in the United States, with United Airlines being one of the most prominent and largest.

3. Former state-owned enterprises under socialist regimes that have been privatized and taken over by their workers in countries like Nicaragua, Russia and parts of eastern Europe.

4. The fair trade campaigns designed to assist small producers, particularly in the third world. A major example is Fair Trade, which labels agricultural products for consumers that are produced by cooperatives and enterprises that adhere to specified labor and environmental standards.

5. Socially responsible investment firms that use environmental and anti-militaristic criteria in making investments, sometimes favoring community-oriented and alternative economic enterprises.

6. Microcredit banks or community funds that make mini-loans to individuals and small-scale enterprises, often in the informal sector of the economy.

7. Community currencies such as the LETS and the Ithaca dollars, in which people at the local level set the values of their services, commodities and labor, exchanging them with one another with these currencies.

8. Land reform movements, such as Brazil's Landless movement, (Sem-Terra) which take over idle or ill-used lands, setting up cooperatives and community activities that provide the infrastructure necessary for the social and economic viability of the new small-scale producers.

9. Small-scale producer agricultural activities and enterprises, particularly in the area of organic agriculture.

10. Marketing and financial cooperatives, many of which have been around for decades.

11. Municipal or community-owned enterprises such as those in southern Brazil, China and even parts of the United States.

12. Autonomous communities with integrated economic and social programs, such as Gaviotas, Colombia, and the communities being organized by the Zapatistas in Chiapas, Mexico.

A major critique of these alternative activities is that many of them are disparate and marginal endeavors that will never be able to challenge the dominant corporate paradigm. However, to understand the growing significance of these activities, they need to be situated in the broader economic and social processes that are taking place. The most important reason why the alternative economies grow in importance is because the very process of globalization marginalizes more and more people as incomes and even jobs are concentrated in fewer and fewer hands, leaving little else for many but the informal economy and alternative economic endeavors.

AN EVOTOPIA?

Aside from marginalization, the centrality of the informational revolution in the globalization process has also opened up new spaces for the conception of alternative economies. Geoffrey Hodgson, in *Economics and Utopia*, argues that some central attributes of capitalism are being undermined by the rise of a knowledge-based economy. Most importantly, the new economy relies more and more on skilled and highly educated workers who require independence and autonomy in the workplace to be effective at their jobs.[3] Owing to this shift, managers and bosses have less of a role in directing the work process. The skilled workers also have far more leverage to negotiate their terms of employment, even, with increasing frequency, obtaining shares or stock options in the companies where they work.

Moreover, some aspects of the information revolution are subverting the nature of commodities and their ownership in a capitalist economy. Many high-tech commodities are less tangible than those of traditional manufacturing. For example, codifiable information products—such as computer programs, CD disks, e-books, e-music, etc.—are difficult for high-tech firms to control as these commodities can be easily reproduced by virtually anyone who obtains a copy. It also becomes more and more questionable whether any given company should have exclusive control of these commodities, as many of them are the product of the accumulated learning and knowledge of society at large. The bio technology companies, for example, rely on science and knowledge developed by universities, by publicly funded projects, such as the research into the human genome, and even more fundamentally, by the stunning, almost exponential growth and spread of knowledge on a global level due to the information revolution itself.

The high-tech corporations have responded to these challenges by pushing for contract, patent and enforcement legislation to prosecute those who reproduce, sell or even give away their products. But these strategies and tactics of control may be stopgap measures or detours as the information economy leads to the ever-wider spread of knowledge. As Hodgson points out, the knowledge economy is inherently democratic, even liberating, as it spreads around the world. Corporate efforts to control it for their own narrow interests often lead to an endless muddle of legislative and litigious maneuvering as the new technologies, skills and products of the information age escape from their control. For example, the corporate music industry sued the startup company Napster to stop its web site from allowing the free downloading and exchange of copyrighted CD music, only to have other Internet sites like Gnutella Web and Freenet spring up to facilitate the free distribution of music.[4] And in Central America, the poorest region in Latin America, there is little the media companies can do to prevent someone with only a minimal education from illicitly hooking up TVs to cable or satellite networks.

Regarding the changes in the workplace, high-tech companies are notoriously anti-union as they try to maintain control of their skilled workers by bargaining with them individually. Many of the high-tech companies also employ a large percentage of temporary workers in order to limit benefits and to keep the skilled workforce off balance and without any basic rights in the company. As Hodgson suggests, a "brave new world of McJobs, unemployment and robots" is one scenario of the information age.[5] A tier of skilled employees could remain subservient to the high-tech corporations, while another broader tier of deskilled and low-paying jobs exists in the economy at large that taps into the large pool of redundant and unemployed workers.

But Hodgson also suggests that in the high-tech workplace "worker knowco ops" may become the wave of the future as the companies seek to attract and keep skilled workers.[6] In this process the internal structures of companies are flattened as workers play a greater role in the management and even the ownership of the firms. Hodgson even suggests that the growing centrality of knowledge in businesses and human endeavors in general could lead to an "Evotopia" in which we gradually evolve into societies that are more democratic while the profit motive becomes one factor among several in determining how we achieve the "common good."[7]

Whether or not an Evotopia or alternative economies gain ascendancy will depend on what controls and demands societies at large are able to exert over the high-tech companies and the knowledge economy. David Korten in *The Post-Corporate World* argues that capitalism, particularly corporate capitalism, has taken control of the market place, creating a global economy that is antithetical to human needs. Corporations dominate markets and pass state legislation that sanctifies their control; there is no "invisible hand" at work as Adam Smith once suggested. Korten argues, however, that "mindful markets" could replace corporate-dominated markets if the public at large asserts its control over the market place, encouraging "diversity, individual initiative and creativity, and productive effort."[8]

Korten lists a number of steps or policies that can lead to mindful markets. One is the empowering of flexible manufacturing networks, such as those that exist in Bologna, Italy, and other parts of Europe, in which networks of small-scale producers are linked together in producers' associations that handle orders and assist in the marketing of goods.[9] It is interesting to note that many large corporations, like Nike, contract out for the manufacturing of the commodities they need with independent firms scattered around the world. This process could be stood on its head if local producers use the web and the networking economy to take control of the marketing and distribution of their products.

Michael Shuman in *Going Local* engages in a detailed study of how to build "self-reliant communities in a global age." He focuses particularly on the financial sector, viewing it as "the starting place for restructuring the local economy" by encouraging the growth of "community banks, thrifts, credit unions and local pension funds." To be successful, the financing and operation of community enterprises requires a shift in government policies to remove "the enormous number of anticommunity subsidies, tax breaks and regulations" that currently favor the corporations and the large banks.[10]

THE SOCIAL CONTEXTUALIZATION OF ALTERNATIVE ECONOMIES

The rise of alternative economies needs to be situated in the broader context of the struggle being waged by the new social movements and grassroots organizations. These movements and activities are taking place in what is called civil society, the ever-expanding array of organizations and networks that function independently of the state. It is in civil society that an almost silent struggle is being waged to form alternative values and practices that challenge the hierarchical and exploitative structures of the corporate and state orders.

The environmental movement, for example, while challenging the ecological destruction of the planet, also encourages and supports alternative economic practices, such as socially responsible investments, and sustainable and organic agriculture. Non-governmental organizations, or NGOs, constitute another major initiative that is flourishing at the grassroots level, independently of states and corporations. NGOs often help foment alternative economic enterprises and fund local social programs and organizations that assist those who are marginalized.

International labor campaigns, such as the support mobilized for the workers organizing at the Han Young assembly plant in Tijuana, Mexico, and the campaign against Nike's third world labor standards, are another part of the broader movement to strengthen the economic rights and participation of those at the bottom. Finally, the campaigns against globalization, such as Fifty Years is Enough, the Jubilee 2000 initiative, led mainly by the churches, and the worldwide call for a tax on international investment transactions (often called the Tobin tax), constitute other campaigns and activities that raise fundamental questions about the existent economic order and create openings for the rise of alternative economies at the grassroots level.

All these diverse economic and social activities are what constitute a virtually existing global revolution. In this new age there is no single agent of social or economic change, such as the working class. Rather, change is carried out by a variety of actors and movements working in the social and economic arenas. The very concept of false consciousness used by Marxists as an explanation for why the working class and the popular sectors are not revolutionary has to be stood on its head. Today those bent on carrying out fundamental changes in our lives and our ways of thinking, such as human rights activists, the feminist, environmental and gay movements, or the churches, have little or no "consciousness" of socialism and Marxism. And yet they, rather than Marxists and self-proclaimed socialists, are having a much more profound effect on societies and peoples around the world.

THE PERSONAL AS THE POSTMODERN POLITICAL

Ultimately, all these alternative movements need to be situated in the context of how individuals can relate to these processes and be the initiators of change. Brian K. Murphy, in *Transforming Ourselves, Transforming the World*, argues that we as individuals have all too often been immobilized and paralyzed by the world around us. In a world dominated by the process of globalization, four basic conditions have produced this paralysis: the breakup of extended family groupings, the communications revolution that makes us feel overwhelmed, the transformation of cultural processes that fragment our existence, and the non-creative structures of modern societies that impose uniformity and make us automatons in a hierarchical order.[11]

To break out of this paralysis, Murphy takes us through a psycho-social analysis of the human condition. If we are to be healthy, he argues, we need to grow, to take risks and, finally, to be activists in the world. In the past, Murphy believes, much of this basic drive for activism had been channeled into political parties or ideologies, which once in power or in control of our lives, imposed a new uniformity and homogeneity.

To breach this historical cul-de-sac, Murphy argues for a "humanist radicalism," a concept borrowed from Eric Fromm.[12] Humanism is neither a Western nor a modern idea; it is as old as human thought. The primary values of humanist radicalism are freedom, growth and health. To be a humanist is to escape from the repression and domination of authoritarian ideologies and religions as well as from rulers who impose their political and cultural norms on us to prevent the realization of the self.

This radical humanist approach can best be actualized in what Murphy calls an "open conspiracy." The word conspiracy comes from the Latin words "to breathe together." As individuals, we can overcome our inertia and powerlessness by conspiring together. This open conspiracy takes as its focus human learning and education. Here Murphy turns to Paulo Freire's belief that education should be "conscientization."[13] Education as an integral part of the open conspiracy combines analysis and action and can take place anywhere and everywhere—in our homes, our churches, our workplaces, our schools, etc. These engagements can enable us to first analyze and understand ourselves and our social realities, and then to take actions to change our lives and the world around us.

In the 1960s the refrain "the personal is the political" was often heard within the New Left and the counter-cultural movement. As we move into the postmodern age, we will need to merge the personal and the political on many different levels in order to create economies and societies that serve human needs rather than the narrow interests and conceits of neo-liberalism and globalization.

THE BATTLE OF SEATTLE AND THE GLOBAL REVOLUTION

Seattle was the coming-out party for a new global movement that merges the personal and the political to challenge the corporate order and "politics as usual." The political parties and distorted ideologies that drove the politics of the twentieth century were largely irrelevant in Seattle, as trade unionists, environmentalists, human rights activists, church groups, AIDS activists, family farmers, and grassroots organizers from around the world collaborated in organizing the marches and demonstrations against the WTO.[14]

The protests represented the culmination of months of an "open conspiracy," involving cooperation and coalition-building among disparate organizations. Many participated in training camps for civil disobedience that were announced on the Internet. The democratic and collective nature of the planning and strategy meetings leading up to the Battle of Seattle created a sense of solidarity and bonding among individuals and organizations from very different backgrounds. Seattle illustrated how the politics of protest are becoming increasingly "de-centered" and yet unified as a wide variety of groups and coalitions come together.

We are witnessing and participating in the formation of a truly diverse global movement capable of challenging the most powerful institutions on the planet. Progressive organizations around the world are drawing up plans for how we can run the global economy with life-centered values instead of accepting the profit- and money-oriented dogmas of the corporate world. The corporate paradigm that is bent on dominating the planet is now losing public support. And the life paradigm, which emphasizes human rights and saving the environment, is gaining acceptance. Transnational unity at the grassroots level is strengthening while the unity of the institutions at the top is fraying, as the disagreements and clashes inside the WTO convention demonstrated.

The various components of this global revolution are all growing vigorously. Look at the world's trade union movement, particularly in the United States. As William Greider notes: "Seattle changed many things, and one of them is American labor."[15] More and more trade unionists are engaging in cross-border solidarity as they realize that organizing within a national context is no longer adequate for dealing with globe-spanning corporations. Trade unions are also expanding their traditionally narrow shop-floor approach, and are replacing it with what is often called social unionism or community-based unionism, which seeks alliances with churches, NGOs, and other organizations in civil society. The victory in Seattle gave this trend a significant boost.

The corporate accountability movement has developed great skill at pressuring corporations to change their objectionable policies, and now the movement is moving up to the next level: questioning the very right of these corporations to exist. People are learning that corporations thrive at our expense because we, the sovereign citizens, charter them and give them a piece of our sovereignty, accepting the absurd fiction that they enjoy the rights of individuals. What can be given can be taken away, if enough citizens demand it. In the United States, people are talking about organizing a campaign to pass an amendment to the U.S. Constitution that says, "a corporation is not a human being," thereby overturning an old Supreme Court ruling that gives corporations the same rights as individuals.

A diverse range of organizations are also working for a return-to-the-local in terms of citizen empowerment. These efforts span the political spectrum from left to right; yet they agree that as much decisionmaking as possible should take place at the local level, where people actually live. This is in sharp contrast to the globalization policies imposed by the likes of the WTO, the IMF and the World Bank. More and more groups are bridging the traditional separation between environmental issues and social justice struggles as they pursue grassroots agendas and strategies.

Activists are going beyond "end-of-pipeline" politics, whereby we react to elite policies by merely trying to soften their impact on people and nature. Instead, we are saying "Let's go inside and change the machinery that is producing bad policy in the first place." It's like the difference between jumping in a river to save each drowning child, and going up-river to get the villain who is throwing the kids in the water in the first place. What these various movements have in common is the goal of expanding the practice of democracy to include the economic realm. They hearken back to the Greek origins of the word democracy—demos meaning people, and kratos meaning rule. It took hundreds of years to achieve the separation of church and state, and now we are in the middle of a long struggle to achieve the separation of corporations and the state.

There will some day be a truly democratic world and a global economy, orchestrated, organized, and run by the diverse societies of the planet. We are only in the early stages of envisioning and creating this new world.

Part Three

Zapatistas and the Latin American Context(ualization)

7 Socialist and Postmodern Politics in the Americas*

To understand the rise of the Zapatista movement it is important to situate it in the context of the collapse of socialism and the emergence of alternative movements in Latin America. The socialist project and socialist ideals largely disintegrated in Latin America with the electoral defeat of the Sandinistas in 1990, the general impasse of the Central American revolutionary movements, and the crisis of Cuban communism following the fall of the Soviet Union. Radical grassroots movements have by no means ended in the Americas, but those that enunciate socialist goals are few and far between. As one commentator on the changes in Latin America has noted: "with the collapse of what could be called the 'grand narratives,' passions were transferred to a huge range and variety of activities that came to be grouped under the ever broader heading of 'social movements' or 'new social movements.'"[1]

During the past four decades there have been four major socialist or neo-socialist experiences in the Americas: Cuba, Chile, Grenada and Nicaragua. The latter two were not self-proclaimed socialist projects, but the processes were anti-imperialist and the governments enacted policies designed to alleviate or eliminate economic and social inequalities. The dominant political parties of these two revolutions—the Sandinista Front and the New Jewel Movement—were imbued with socialist concepts and ideals.

The reasons for the failure or demise of each of these experiences are varied, although if there is one overriding cause it is that the other metanarrative of the twentieth century, capitalism and its dominant agent, U.S. imperialism, proved to be far more flexible and adaptive, developing a variety of interventionary strategies in the economic, social and political spheres. Interestingly, it was not direct military intervention that defeated any of them. The 1961 invasion of Cuba at the Bay of Pigs was an abysmal failure and led to the consolidation of Cuban socialism, while the U.S. invasion of Grenada

* Parts of this chapter originally appeared in the NACLA *Report on the Americas*, "Socialism is Dead, Long Live Socialism", November–December, 1997.

in 1983 came only after the revolutionary movement had self-destructed and executed its own leaders.

Of course, the four socialist experiences under consideration had very different strengths and weaknesses that contributed to their ultimate failure. To understand just how the U.S. succeeded and what the implications are for any future radical social project we need to scrutinize each process. The general thesis presented here is that twentieth-century socialism in the Americas failed for two contradictory reasons: in those socialist experiences that were the most democratic, like Chile during 1970–73, the U.S. was able to exploit their relatively open political and economic processes to destroy them from within. On the other hand, in those societies with more centralized and vertical structures, exemplified principally by Cuba, the lack of authentic democratic processes weakened their mass base, led to popular alienation, produced inefficient state-dominated economies and provided gist for the ongoing U.S. ideological campaign against communism and socialism. To put it in postmodern terminology, one could argue that the Chilean experience was more open-ended and less rigidly structured as a metanarrative, whereas the Cuban model was more absolute, and thus unable to accommodate the innumerable specificities of its own peoples, thereby eventually alienating them from the political process.

Caught on the horns of this dilemma, twentieth-century socialism in the Americas was probably destined to eventual failure since its inception. Only by constructing entirely new radical narratives from the ground up can the contradictory weakness of classical, twentieth-century socialism be surmounted.

THE EPOCHAL SHIFT AND SOCIALIST REVOLUTIONS

Yet before a new approach can be postulated, we need to understand the nature of late capitalism and imperialism. Here, as argued in the earlier chapters, the starting point is that in recent years capitalism has undergone an epochal shift with globalization. This shift has altered the political paradigm that the core countries are advocating for the third world. As William Robinson shows in *Promoting Polyarchy*, in order to integrate the third world into a global neo-liberal economy the United States has turned against many of the dictators it once nurtured and adopted a policy of supporting, and even imposing, controlled democracies.[2]

The U.S. effort to oust Pinochet in Chile in the late 1980s was the first manifestation of this new policy approach in the hemisphere. More recently, the invasion of Haiti to reinstall Jean-Bertrand Aristide served as a dramatic illustration of this policy shift. In general, the U.S. and the other imperial powers now recognize that dictators, because they seek to control their economies as well as their societies for their own narrow interests, are politically unstable and do not provide the best terrain for the advance of corporate trade and transnational capital.

This approach does not prevent the U.S. from endorsing pseudo-democratic regimes, such as that of Alberto Fujimori in Peru, which shut down the Congress in 1992, ruled by emergency decree and then adopted a new constitution that gave Fujimori virtual dictatorial powers. But it is important to note that, even in these instances, the regimes do hold referendums and elections that give them a certain sense of legitimacy, both domestically and internationally. And in the 2000 campaign, when Fujimori tried to rig the election for a third term, the Clinton administration made it clear that electoral fraud would not be accepted.

The implications of this epochal shift for the future of radical struggles in Latin America and elsewhere are many. For one, it means that building an alternative movement around a vertical Marxist-Leninist state or political party will never again be effective. Imperialism, especially U.S. imperialism, is now extremely adept at using the language, and even the basic forms of democracy to advance the interests of the transnational elites. Radical movements for change can only be successful to the extent that they are able to show that they are more democratic and open-ended in their struggles and goals than the neo-liberal democratic paradigm. In particular, they need to continually demonstrate that true democracy extends to the economic arena and that the unregulated market advocated by neo-liberals is incompatible with authentic democracy. Neo-liberalism is in effect a metanarrative or absolutist paradigm that constricts the potential of individuals and societies outside the market place.[3]

The growing awareness among progressives and radicals of the importance of transparent elections and basic political freedoms explains why Cuba in recent years has ceased to serve as a model for popular struggles in the Americas. It is not the economic difficulties

Cuba is experiencing nor the U.S. blockade that has weakened the appeal of Cuba. In fact, the Cuban standard of living and its economic plight were much more severe in the late 1960s than they are in the 1990s. But in the 1960s the revolution enjoyed extensive popular support because Cubans had a sense that they were participating in the political and economic life of their country. This was a revolutionary metanarrative, but it was open-ended and very flexible, engaging in constant experimentation. However, during the 1970s the Cuban communist party and the state consolidated control over virtually all facets of the economy and exercised centralized control over the trade unions, the educational system and "mass organizations," like the women's association.

In recent years in Cuba there has been a devolution of many state enterprises to worker- and peasant-run cooperatives, particularly in the agricultural sphere. But few steps have been taken to democratize the country, as Fidel Castro and the party insist on retaining absolute political power. The Cuban variant of socialism may survive into the foreseeable future, but until the political system opens up the revolution will remain in a largely defensive position, unable to provide inspiration for a renewal of socialism in the Americas.

SANDINISTAS ON THE CUSP

The Sandinista revolutionary leadership was on the cusp of a new politics. It understood to a large extent that the old socialist paradigm of a single party state was no longer viable and that democratic elections were necessary. Thus, the Sandinistas, instead of monopolizing political power, brought other parties into the process in a coalition government and held open elections, beginning in 1984. And, on the economic front, the Sandinista Front advocated a "mixed economy," one with some enterprises controlled by the state while other parts of the economy remained in the hands of private interests.

But, in a certain sense, the Sandinista revolution was fatally caught between the new and the old: while allowing pluralist elections the Sandinista Front was a vanguard centralist party with a "national directorate" that exercised tight control not only over the party, but also over the affiliated "mass" or social movements. And, on the economic front, many of the state enterprises were very inefficiently run with limited worker or peasant participation. At the same time, the other parts of the economic and political spheres that were completely autonomous were in a position to undermine or sabotage Sandinista initiatives.

In the end the U.S. and its allies inside and outside of Nicaragua proved to be adept at tarring the Sandinistas with the "totalitarian" brush while manipulating public opinion and civil society. They forged an alternative counter-revolutionary bloc in Nicaragua comprised of a number of political parties, civic and business organizations, the Catholic hierarchy, and even trade unions and sectors of the peasantry. This coalition brought Violeta Chamorro to power in 1990.

THE CHILEAN TRAGEDY

In Chile it was not sectarianism, verticalism or the lack of democracy that destroyed the Popular Unity coalition that governed Chile during 1970–73, but Nixon's and Kissinger's "invisible blockade." Certainly, there were political squabbles and differences that hampered the coalition at times, but it was fundamentally the blockade that crippled the economy, destabilized the political system, and laid the basis for the U.S.-backed coup by General Augusto Pinochet.[4]

The government of Salvador Allende made one fatal mistake—its failure in mid-1973 to retain General Prats as head of the military and to purge the officers who were conspiring against him. Such a move would probably also have required the arming of working-class civilians and the overnight creation of popular militias to fight with the loyalist sectors of the military. However, as Allende realized, a decision to back Prats with these measures would have provoked a civil war and required the suspension of the Chilean parliament and constitution. These measures were abhorrent to Allende and to most of the parties of the Popular Unity coalition, given their commitment to maintaining Chile's democratic institutions. It was this paradoxical choice between maintaining the Popular Unity's commitment to established democratic rules and procedures and the need to take military steps to destroy the opposition that makes Chile the most tragic socialist experience in the Americas and perhaps in the history of twentieth-century socialism.

One thesis put forth by some former Popular Unity militants in Chile today is that the economic policies of the Allende government played a critical role in its demise. This is a dubious argument as most of the economic difficulties were due to the blockade and economic sabotage by the domestic bourgeoisie. Aside from the workers' takeover of many state industries, the macro-economic policies of the Popular Unity government were quite similar to those of the previous Christian Democratic government of Eduardo Frei. Import substitution, industrialization, agrarian reform, the "Chileanization" of foreign-dominated sectors of the economy like the copper industry, and significant deficit financing with high rates of inflation—these were economic policies that characterized both the Frei and Allende governments. By 1973 the Chilean economy was experiencing hyperinflation, but this was due to the blockade and a domestic deadlock in the Chilean Congress that hampered any legislation, including fiscal and taxation measures. Moreover, other governments in Latin America in the 1970s experienced hyperinflation without being overthrown.

The current center-left government of Chile led by Ricardo Lagos of the Socialist Party rejects the economic policies of the Allende government and basically endorses a free market economy. For Lagos and other governments in Latin America, even Keynesian policies are considered unviable in the era of globalization as any efforts to restrict or control the flow of international capital by a given government are immediately met by capital flight and economic crisis. The argument of some Latin American leftists against any effort to revive socialist economic policies is perhaps best encapsulated in Jorge Castaneda's book, *Utopia Unarmed*. He asserts that the left, particularly in Latin America, has to accept "the logic of the market" and limit itself to choosing what type of capitalist system it buys into, whether neo-liberal, or closer to the more socially oriented models of western Europe or Japan.[5]

THE RESURGENCE OF RURAL MOVEMENTS

At this point in history, the left, instead of buying into the globalization process on its own terms, can draw inspiration from the many local, popular movements occurring throughout the Americas that erupted after the demise of socialism. Among the peasantry and indigenous populations of Latin America, there is a renewed insurgency as demonstrated by the landless movement in Brazil, the struggles of the coca farmers in Bolivia, the rebellion of the Mapuches in Chile, the Zapatista insurrection of Chiapas, and the Indian uprisings in Ecuador. These movements draw support from, and are even linked to, urban movements.[6] Indeed, many of the new leaders of these movements have some relationship to the urban areas, often having gone to the cities to look for work or to educate themselves.

In Ecuador, the new millennium began with an indigenous uprising that ousted the corrupt neo-liberal government of Jamil Mahuad on January 21, 2000. The Indians were led by the Indigenous Nationalities Confederation of Ecuador (CONAIE), which occupied parliament and allied itself with a sector of the military to set up a civilian-military triumvirate. CONAIE, comprised of twelve Indian nations that represent 45 per cent of Ecuador's population, called for an end to the country's neo-liberal economic policies and the creation of a multinational state in which the Indian nations would have economic and political autonomy. The confederation also advocated "popular parliaments" in which people could directly present their grievances and compel the government to respond to their needs.[7]

This program of authentic democracy was unacceptable to the U.S. government and the Organization of American States. They intervened diplomatically to compel the military to back out of its alliance with the Indians and to install the vice-president in power, who continued most of Mahuad's policies, including the dollarization of the Ecuadorian economy. In the aftermath of the coup, however, polls indicated that CONAIE retained the support of over 70 per cent of Ecuadorians. Committed to non-violence, the president of CONAIE, Antonio Vargas, stated on February 4, 2000:

> Many people were excited that power was in our hands [in January], but to exercise this power is difficult. That is why we say it is better things turned out as they did. And with this experience we now have to prepare ourselves even more, training professionals, strengthening our alliances with other social sectors and continuing to promote the unity of the movement. In the long term we have a dream of profound changes in this country that will benefit all of society.[8]

ALTERNATIVE ECONOMIES

As Vargas's statement indicates, these peasant and indigenous struggles in Latin America are more than defensive. The landless movement in Brazil is developing alternative economic projects, securing international funding, often from non-governmental organizations, or NGOs. And, for the Zapatistas of Mexico, a central plank of their struggle is that the indigenous communities of Chiapas are entitled to the resources necessary to carry out their own autonomous economic development. These are important self-help approaches, calculated to develop alternative, viable economies at the local and regional levels.

The alternative economies discussed in the previous chapter exist throughout Latin America. They are comprised of highly differentiated activities and economic islands that rise phoenix-like out of what capitalism discards. Perhaps the most extensive of these economies in Latin America consists of the informal sector—the ever more numerous street venders, flea markets, petty family businesses, and even garbage scavengers who recycle aluminum cans, cardboard and bottles while using what they can of the refuse. On a larger scale, another alternative economic sector is comprised of privately owned enterprises, like some of the plantations in Central America that are taken over or sold off to peasants, agricultural cooperatives or small-scale producers because the often depressed international prices of sugar, cotton and bananas make these lands marginally useful for the oligarchs and *latifundistas*. These are all nascent, alternative economic activities because they represent efforts by people to take control of their lives at the most fundamental, grassroots level.[9]

Here the ongoing struggles of peasants and workers in post-Sandinista Nicaragua—which have been devastated by neo-liberal governments and the natural disaster of Hurricane Mitch—are particularly instructive. Over 350 enterprises of all sizes and types, many of which were controlled by the state under the Sandinista government, are owned and run by the workers. When the Chamorro government began to sell them off as part of the privatization process demanded by the IMF and the World Bank, the workers on many of these enterprises simply occupied them, and/or began to negotiate for taking control of them. Today there is a national association of worker-run enterprises that facilitates their development and access to technical assistance and capital while lobbying with the government and the banks for their growth and expansion into new areas of the economy.[10]

All these areas of postmodern economic activity are growing in importance in Latin America and the Caribbean, not because they can compete in any significant way with transnational capital, but because they are the only option available to ever-increasing numbers of people. A subcontractor for a large corporation, a refuse scavenger, a worker-run cooperative, a micro-entrepreneur in the informal economy, a peasant or a street vendor—none of them abandon their activities because there is little else they can do to survive.

The alternative economies and their participants will continue to grow in importance because global capitalism excludes more and more people, and also because of inherent crises and contradictions within the system itself. Clearly, these new economies need to advance in tandem with alternative political movements and with the struggles of workers and peasants. Popular economies can survive and grow even in the midst of a globalized world only if people become increasingly conscious of their need to struggle for them, building a "new politics" along with new economic activities.

THE NEW SOCIAL MOBILIZATIONS

Here the EZLN and the Zapatistas in Chiapas are particularly illustrative of how this process can unfold. Their political and economic demands are focused largely on the needs of Chiapas and its indigenous peoples. This is probably the first national liberation movement that did not proclaim as its objective a march on the capital city and the seizure of total power. Rather, the Zapatistas have focused on civil society as the agent of change, calling for the mobilization of a wide array of civic associations and organizations to demand authentic economic and political democracy. The strength of the Zapatistas has not come from the "barrel of a gun,"—in fact, at times they have had only wooden guns—but from their ability to capture the hearts and minds of Mexican society and the international community, to effectively wage a political-ideological war against the PRI and the Mexican state.

Even at the level of the state, new challenges to the traditional systems of "democratic" rule are emerging. Hugo Chavez in Venezuela has tossed out the old political order and written a new constitution with massive public support. Few new economic policies were announced during the first year of his government, due in part to the floods that devastated large parts of the country in early 2000 and created a national emergency. But Chavez did end the harsh neo-liberal policies of his predecessors, refusing to privatize the oil industry and to impose any more fiscal austerity programs on the backs of the poor. The future of Chavez's experiment will depend on whether he empowers the different social sectors to take control of their own lives at the grassroots level, or becomes little more than a *caudillo*, accumulating more and more power in his own hands.

The arrest and detention of Augusto Pinochet in London in October 1998 transformed the political atmosphere in much of Latin America. Military and dictatorial leaders have been put on notice that they are responsible for crimes committed against their own citizens. Although Pinochet escaped the Spanish tribunals for alleged health reasons, he returned to Chile a discredited figure, facing prosecution and endless legal challenges in the Chilean courts. The application of international law to former rulers and heads of state represents an historic victory for the human rights movement. It is one of the more critical new social movements that are shaking the established political and legal orders from the bottom up.

Earlier in Chile, the development of a broadly-based human rights movement with a strong feminist component was instrumental in forcing the Pinochet regime to relinquish power in 1990. However, the U.S. government contained the popular movement by backing a transitional accord that recognized the constitution of the Pinochet regime, including the clauses that provided for military autonomy and a number of senators-for-life in the Chilean Congress, including Pinochet and the heads of the three branches of the Chilean military.

With the election of Lagos, the human rights movement in Chile is agitating for the prosecution of Pinochet, an end to the "authoritarian enclaves" in the constitution, and the expansion of human rights to other arenas of Chilean economic and social life. Just one week after Lagos's inauguration in March 2000 a music concert was held at Santiago's National Stadium that drew more than 50,000 people to raise funds for a memorial center dedicated to the victims of the Pinochet regime. The crowd for the concert was comprised overwhelmingly of people in their teens and twenties who chanted and jeered at every mention of Pinochet.

Viviena Diaz, the president of the Organization of the Families of the Detained and Disappeared that convened the concert, made it clear that many Chileans are intent on building a new Chile that goes beyond the prosecution of Pinochet. "We want health care, education, work, housing, justice and human rights," she proclaimed. "We will support the Lagos government when it is implementing these rights; we will criticize when it doesn't."[11]

In the introduction to a NACLA report "Voices on the Left," which contains interviews with activists from around the hemisphere, the NACLA editors note that it is "all the more remarkable ... that in this age of doubt and cynicism, the activists interviewed .. maintain a radical commitment and enthusiasm." The NACLA Report declared that these dissidents "are not lone voices in the wilderness but social activists engaged in the struggles of their times and places. There is an emphasis ... on democratic modes of development, mass partici-pation in politics and structural, 'achievable' reforms."[12]

This constitutes a new politics in Latin America, a politics that is part of the virtually existing global revolution. It is a revolution with many local agendas, a revolution with a hundred faces and experi-ences, a revolution without a formal name or a grand narrative at present. As Bishop Samuel Ruiz of Chiapas says, "The Zapatistas emerged without faces because they represent many unseen faces from elsewhere which are now emerging as new subjects."[13] The genius of these struggles is that every effort to raise consciousness or to develop self-help projects at the local level is innately part of the long-term process of building new alternatives. They exist here and now, even if capitalism retains control of the global economy and the formal political systems.

8   Roots of the Postmodern Rebellion in Chiapas*

The Zapatista rebellion is the first postmodern revolutionary movement. For many, including *New York Times* correspondents, the initial conception of the movement in 1994 as postmodern arose from its Internet communiqués and its adroit use of the media.[1] But a number of other tendencies soon emerged to make it a new type of political movement. This was not a single-minded revolt of indigenous peoples who merely wanted to retake their lands and expel the rich who exploited them. Here was a rebellion that consciously sought to move beyond the politics of modernity, be they of past national liberation movements, or of the repressive "modernization" policies of the Mexican government.

The uprising led by the Zapatista National Liberation Army, (or EZLN as it is known by its Spanish acronym), occurred in the wake of the collapse of the "modern" bipolar world of the post-World War II era and the ideological exhaustion of most national liberation movements. What distinguishes the EZLN from its predecessors is that it has not sought power in Mexico City, nor is it calling for state socialism. Its objective throughout the 1990s was to spark a broadly-based movement of civil society in Chiapas and the rest of Mexico that will transform the country from the bottom up.

Internally, the EZLN has moved beyond the democratic centralist structure of past national liberation movements that resulted in more centralism than democracy. The very structure of the EZLN is fluid, with a clandestine committee in charge of day-to-day operations that is consultative and has a policy of rotating members.[2] The EZLN goes to great lengths to involve the local communities in the organization's decisionmaking process, whether it be the discussion of negotiations with the Mexican government or basic decisions of making war and peace.

The EZLN also breaks with the tradition of the "heroic" guerrilla commanders. EZLN leaders downplay their individual roles,

* An earlier version of this chapter appeared in *New Left Review*, No. 205, May–June 1994.

mocking the pretentiousness of many leaders of other national liberation movements, as is evident in the title "Sub-Comandante" Marcos, the *nom de guerre* assumed by its well-known public spokesperson. Marcos has certainly been the most notable figure of the movement, but this has been due not to his control or command of the movement but to his literary and communication skills, which have caused the Mexican and the international media to focus on his personality. Two of the internal principles of the EZLN are that its leaders cannot own property or hold political office, principles that differentiate it sharply from other national liberation organizations, like the Sandinistas of Nicaragua. Marcos, in adhering to these principles, not only has no residence and sleeps wherever nightfall finds him, but has turned over all royalties from his publications to Zapatista communities and to public charities in Mexico.

The postmodernity and advanced politics of the rebellion is rooted in part in the movement's awareness of the dramatic changes occurring on the world scene and the past limitations of national liberation movements. But even more importantly it is the product of the political and social struggle that has been taking place in Chiapas for decades. The uprising is fundamentally a rebellion against capitalism and the political economy of modernization that the Mexican government has sought to impose on Chiapas as well as the rest of the country.

Contrary to popular conception, Chiapan society is not a provincial backwater nor is the economy of the state neo-feudal. The Indians and peasants of Chiapas are deeply aware that they are the victims of modernization. Over the past quarter of a century the economy of Chiapas has been transformed by capitalism. The popular forces in the state, Indian and peasant alike, have been compelled to react and organize to deal with this profound upheaval. Their demands for change have become postmodern in that they want a new social and economic order that goes beyond capitalism while also rejecting the twentieth-century socialist project.

THE POVERTY OF PROGRESS IN CHIAPAS

One of the most striking characteristics of the state of Chiapas is its wealth. Chiapas occupies only 3.8 per cent of Mexico's land surface, and has about three and a half million inhabitants out of a total Mexican population of about 90 million. But this state produces over half of Mexico's hydro-electric power, is the second largest petroleum producing state and the largest coffee exporter. Chiapas is also the third largest producer of corn, the fifth biggest cattle producer (until recently it was second), and it numbers among the top three Mexican states in tobacco, banana, soy and cacao production.[3] And although the Chiapan rain forests have been ravaged over the decades, the state still remains the second largest producer of lumber in Mexico.

This striking wealth stands in contrast to the abject poverty of the Chiapan. It has the worst indices of poverty and marginalization of Mexico's 32 states. About three-quarters of its people are malnourished, half of them live in dwellings with only dirt floors, 19 per cent of the economically active population receive no income, while another 39 per cent earn less than the minimum wage, which is about $3 a day.[4]

The state's official statistics claim that the infant mortality rate is about 39 per thousand, the same as the national average. But an independent study in Chiapas found that most infant deaths in Indian villages simply go unreported to the authorities, and that the real infant mortality rate is 54.7 per thousand.[5] Mortality rates among all age groups in Chiapas are high due to infections, malnutrition, anemia, and many diseases that are preventable with vaccinations.

About 30 per cent of the children do not go to school. And, for a large portion of those who do, schooling is characterized by low attendance rates and poorly motivated teachers who have little interest in working in small communities, or who, worse still, have no capacity to speak the primary Indian language of most of the students. In some cases children attend school for six years and receive their primary degree without really knowing Spanish, the only language they were ever taught in.

This contrast between extreme wealth and poverty in Chiapas is in large part the result of the capitalist revolution that has ravaged the state. Over the past quarter of a century Chiapas has been convulsed by unprecedented economic transformations that have torn up the traditional agricultural economy and devastated the indigenous cultures. The Mexican state, responding to the interests of the country's emergent bourgeoisie and the demands of the international market place, has treated Chiapas as an internal colony, sucking out its wealth while leaving its people—particularly the overwhelming majority who live off the land—more impoverished than ever.

THE NEO-COLONIAL BACKDROP

In 1970 it was not apparent that Chiapas would soon experience an economic boom that would accentuate the state's extremes of wealth and poverty. As Luis Echeverria took power in Mexico City in 1970—the eighth president in succession belonging to the ruling PRI party—Chiapas was locked in a social and economic system that retained many of the characteristics of the colonial era.

To be sure, this was a system already marked by inequalities and exploitation. The highland Indian communities, largely located in the region around the old provincial city of San Cristobal de las Casas, had for centuries constituted the principal labor force for the extraction of Chiapan resources. Steeped in a communal religious system based on a syncretism of Christian and Mayan beliefs, the Indians grew staple crops on their village *milpas*, or plots of land, and held corn, their principal staple, as an almost sacred crop. The highland Indian communities, due to coercion, debt servitude and population pressures, also provided workers to open up the rest of this geographically diverse state, which contained rich river valleys, tropical rain forests, Sierra mountain ranges, and fertile coastal plains next to the Pacific Ocean.

As of 1970 the nearby Grijalva river basin was a major area of migration as many highland Indians journeyed down the Pan American highway (opened in 1947) to rent lands to augment the meager crops produced on their own village lands. Other Indians migrated annually to harvest coffee, either in the Sierran areas near the highlands or by going southwest to the Pacific coast where some of the state's richest plantations were found. On these estates, the Indians would also harvest bananas, sugar cane, cotton and other crops.

For well over a century the highland Indians had also been moving in the opposite directions, north and east, towards the jungle areas and the Lacandon rain forest.[6] There, depending on the particular commodity that was in favor on the world market, the Indians would harvest indigo, hardwoods, rubber, cacao and coffee. During the 1950s and 1960s, beef cattle became the principal agricultural endeavor of the region. Indians would first move in to clear the land, often growing corn for a few years, only to be replaced by ranchers. At other times the Indians would immediately establish grazing areas for cattle ranching to take over. By 1970 the burgeoning beef cattle industry had already destroyed much of the rain forest area.

In the highlands as well as the rest of the state, the Mexican revolution and a succession of PRI presidents had made important changes in the system of exploitation. During the late 1930s and early 1940s agrarian reform finally came to Chiapas, leading to the breakup of many of the old *latifundia* that had served as the backbone of the oligarchy's control of the state over the centuries.[7] As of 1950 Indian communities in many of the highland towns had gained control over half of the land or more, forming *ejidos*, or communal farms.

But the best lands, particularly in the cleared rain forests, the Grijalva Valley, and on the Pacific coast remained under the control of an elite of wealthy farmers, plantation owners, and *nouveau riche* ranchers. And, even in the highlands, many of the old *latifundia* owners only ceded their more marginal lands to the Indian communities. As permitted by the law, they kept the choicest property (often up to 3,000 hectares) for themselves, including the machinery, buildings and agricultural processing facilities. In many cases the family estates were actually larger as each member of the family placed tracts of land in his or her name, thereby evading the law. In some ways, the parceling out of lands actually helped the oligarchs stabilize their labor force as the Indians could not produce enough on their own marginal plots and were compelled to augment their income by serving as common laborers on the nearby estates.

In the highland areas as well as the rest of the state, a group of *caciques*, or powerful intermediaries, aligned themselves with the ruling PRI to manipulate the bureaucracies and to turn local politics to their advantage. The *caciques* were usually mestizoes or ladinos, but many were Indians. Some would be appointed as municipal presidents by the state governor, others would gain control of key properties and assets that they used as a source of local power, and still others would manipulate local credit, commerce and transportation facilities, extracting their cut in exchange for "assistance" or protection. The *caciques* helped ensure that the Indians would be kept in line, providing a constant and stable workforce for the state's agricultural economy. In effect, the *caciques* greased the wheels of a system that still favored the rich and well-to-do, be they in Mexico City, San Cristobal de las Casas, or in the provincial towns dominated by ranchers and businessmen.

Although battered over the ages by one conquering or exploiting group after another, the Indian communities in 1970 still maintained a certain resilience. Indeed, the highland Chiapas area had become a favored area of study for anthropologists seeking to understand indigenous communities. The Harvard anthropological project in particular sent out a number of researchers to chronicle the farming techniques, religious beliefs, and communal values of the Tzotzil and Tzeltal Indians who were predominant in the highlands. One of the anthropologists' central research themes was that of trying to understand how these Indians had held onto their own values and lifestyles in spite of centuries of exploitation and domination by outside forces.[8]

THE CAPITALIST ONSLAUGHT

What came to differentiate the decade of the Seventies from the previous periods of exploitation in Chiapas was the intensity of the process of capitalist exploitation that took hold. The Chiapan economy boomed during the 1970s, growing at an annual rate of 10.5 per cent. Cattle ranching and export crops were the driving forces behind the agricultural transformation of the state. In 1970, Chiapas had two million head of cattle; by 1980 the figure had risen to 3.8 million and by 1983 it peaked at 4 million.[9] Export crops, like bananas and cotton, also grew rapidly, doubling their total production during the decade. In 1970 Chiapas produced 7.7 per cent of Mexico's agricultural crop exports: by 1980 its share stood at 12.4 per cent.[10]

The onslaught of cattle raising was particularly destructive. Based on extensive grazing, the Chiapan cattle industry fomented the concentration and monopolization of land, the displacement of traditional agricultural crops, the continued destruction of the rain forest, and the illegal occupation and renting of *ejido*, or communal, lands by large cattle producers. As a result, by 1983, 30 per cent of Chiapan lands were once again controlled by *latifundistas* while at least 100,000 peasants were landless.[11]

During the 1970s the Mexican government and the World Bank encouraged *ejidos* and peasants to participate in cattle production, largely through credit programs. But instead of assisting the small producers, this actually reinforced the power of the large cattle barons and accelerated the process of capital accumulation within the cattle industry. In effect, the *campesinos* and *ejidatarios* occupied a subordinate and risky position in the cattle production chain. They usually raised calves, which were sold to the large ranchers to fatten up on their extensive grazing lands. The small calf producers incurred substantial losses due to disease, poor sanitation facilities, insufficient technical assistance and a lack of genetic improvement programs. Moreover, the smaller producers had limited markets, often being compelled to sell their calves to the local cattle baron at the price he dictated. Faced with heavy losses and few profits, it is no wonder that by the late 1970s many *campesinos* and *ejidos* actually preferred to rent their lands to large cattle owners, thereby accentuating the process of land concentration in the state.[12]

THE PETROLEUM BOOM

The other locus of capitalist development was the petroleum industry in northeastern Chiapas. Exploration and drilling was carried out during 1969–71, and during the remainder of the 1970s oil and natural gas production boomed. The emergence of this industry dramatically altered the Chiapan social and economic scene. While the engineers, managers and skilled personnel were brought in from outside the state by PEMEX (the government-owned petroleum company), thousands of Chiapan peasants came to the northeast to work in the menial jobs of construction, maintenance and transportation.[13]

The northeastern petroleum enclave soon became a glaring social sore in the state of Chiapas. Agricultural lands and production in the area were destroyed and the peasant population uprooted.[14] Moreover, like most boom town areas, the living conditions were substandard. Dramatic increases occurred in the indices of prostitution, violence, crime and alcoholism. There was a lack of housing and public services, while prices for basic goods skyrocketed, touching off an inflationary spiral that affected the entire state.

The problems precipitated by the petroleum, cattle and export booms were accentuated by the building of hydro-electric dams on the Grijalva river during the 1970s. The new reservoirs flooded over 100,000 hectares of some of the best lands in Chiapas while another 100,000 hectares were lost due to micro-climatic changes and the isolation of large stretches of land. About 90,000 people were forced to move, placing new pressures on the remaining lands of Chiapas.[15]

THE SOCIAL UPHEAVAL

The onslaught of these transformations precipitated a profound social upheaval throughout Chiapas. A complex array of forces came into play that included the federal government, Church liberation theologists, independent peasant organizations, growing social and economic differentiation within the Indian and peasant communities, and the use of violence by ranchers, *caciques*, and governors of the state bent on retaining their economic privileges.

Luis Echeverria, who served as president during 1970–76, actually sought to modernize the system of economic and political exploitation by imposing a neo-corporatist regime on the state. To break the power of the *caciques*, who came to be viewed as detrimental to the Mexican state's ability to siphon off resources at the national level, government-run commercial institutions were set up to provide credit and buy coffee, corn and other commodities directly from the small producers, thereby bypassing the *caciques* and local *intermediarios* or merchants. The Echeverria government also stepped up social spending in Chiapas, albeit in a manner that sought to make local communities beholden to federal and PRI party officials at the expense of local power brokers.

Echeverria's shaking of the old establishment at the top helped to open up space for new social movements to seize the initiative from below. Key to this process was the spread of liberation theology. In 1974, Archbishop Samuel Ruiz, at the suggestion of Echeverria, sponsored an Indian congress in San Cristobal de las Casas that brought together over 1,000 communities, representing 400,000 people. Ruiz insisted on total autonomy for the congress, out of which came a series of resolutions denouncing the miserable conditions of Indian life and, even more importantly, creating the first independent, statewide network of Indian communities since the conquest. *Catequistas*, disciples of the social gospel and liberation theology, were central to this process as they went from community to community discussing the system of oppression and precipitating a sense of empowerment among the Indians.[16]

Other, more overtly political forces also became active in Chiapas. In the mid-1970s left-wing student activists, the product of the university rebellion in 1968, began organizing among the peasants. A few years later, more formal political organizations, including some with links to the Mexican Communist Party, began setting up peasant organizations like the Independent Central of Agricultural Workers and Peasants (CIOAC). A Maoist group also began organizing cooperatives of small coffee producers that soon led to a union of 150 community *ejidos*, primarily in the Lacandon rain forest.[17]

This extensive organizing led to a virtual explosion of activity in the 1970s, and by the early 1980s there were revolts or protests in over half of the municipalities of Chiapas.[18] Violent conflicts became commonplace, particularly over land. Scores of people were killed as local landowners, government troops and *guardias blancas* (hired gunmen of the ranchers) sought to end land occupations and break up public demonstrations.

The situation became so explosive that in early 1983 President Miguel de la Madrid, just months after taking office, made an emergency trip to Chiapas. His efforts were aimed at containing and controlling the growing social upheaval. He first set up a commission to deal with land tenancy disputes, and then placed the state under strict military control.[19] The state governor he appointed, General Absalon Castellanos Dominguez, launched an extensive land reform program that granted large blocks of land primarily to *ejidos* and Indian communities. By the time he left the governor's office in 1988, more land had been distributed in Chiapas than in the previous 30 years.[20]

The land reform program, however, did nothing to alleviate conflict in the state. The government's strategy in distributing land was to ignore or undermine independent peasant and Indian organizations that had fought for the land while favoring groups and organizations that had been acquiescent or aligned with the PRI, like the National Confederation of Campesinos (CNC). Of 493 major land grants made in the state, only 27 went to communities or *ejidos* aligned with militant peasant organizations.[21] In many cases, the CNC, knowing which lands the government was about to expropriate, would arm peasants aligned with it or use the police to move in and violently expel independent peasant organizations that were already occupying the lands.

Castellanos Dominguez also did his best to ensure the security of those ranchers and large landowners that remained. As in past reforms, the large landowners that were affected by agrarian reform retained the prime lands for themselves. Many others were not touched and even special decrees were issued exempting them from any future land expropriations. By 1988 about 70 per cent of the cattle ranches in the state were officially exempted from land reform.[22]

This intensified conflict in the state took place against the backdrop of a national economic crisis that had severe repercussions for Chiapas. In 1982 the drop in petroleum prices and the onset of the debt crisis forced the Mexican government to devalue the currency and to enact an austerity program that went on for the remainder of the decade. As a result, petroleum production plummeted in Chiapas, and the agricultural system was shaken.

The slashing of government-sponsored credits for agriculture had a particularly debilitating effect. In Chiapas the production of corn between 1982 and 1987 fell by almost 20 per cent, while that of beans dropped by 18 per cent. But other cash and export crops boomed, due largely to the devaluation of the peso and the resulting higher earnings of cash crops on the international market. The production of soybeans, peanuts, sorghum and tobacco during the period grew by 150.8, 244.1, 144.8 and 261.2 per cent respectively, while the output of cacao and sugar cane doubled. Banana production displayed only a "modest" growth of 25 per cent.[23] The amount of beef marketed increased by 400 per cent from 1982 to 1987, although the size of the state's cattle herd dropped by 22 per cent, indicating that ranchers were liquidating their herds in order to reap immediate profits.[24]

THE NEW CLASS SOCIETY

The increasing orientation of agriculture towards the international markets combined with the onslaught of capitalism throughout Chiapas, had dramatically altered class relations within the peasant and Indian communities by the late 1980s. Peasants who had accumulated some earnings as workers in the petroleum fields or who had in one way or another been able to build up savings during the boom period, began to use their small capital to invest in green revolution technologies. This soon led to pronounced class stratification within even the traditional Indian villages.

One study of the highland Indian community of Zinacatan presented to the United Nations Research Institute for Social Development shows how many of the young Zinacantecos who returned home from the petroleum fields invested in fertilizers and herbicides to grow corn. As the study points out:

Before, Zinacantecos had deployed household members in labour-intensive cultivation, giving advantage to elders who could subordinate youthful kin. Today as Zinacantecos purchase and use chemical fertilizer and weed sprays, their farming has become much less labour-intensive and more to the advantage of those who control commercial transport and capital. The work of the field hand has become more of a commodity to be bought and sold, to the advantage of a class of youthful men who have brought new wealth—derived from construction contracting, commerce, and trucking—into farming.[25]

The neo-liberal modernization policies of President Salinas de Gortari (1988–94) accelerated the process of class stratification, impoverishment and conflict throughout Chiapas. Virtually all vestiges of reformist policies implemented by previous PRI presidents to try to contain the growing discontent in Chiapas were terminated. INMECAFE, the state agency set up under Echeverria to purchase coffee and set prices to assist small coffee producers, was abolished, leading to the virtual collapse of small-scale coffee production in Chiapas between 1989 and 1993.

Corn, the key commodity of Chiapas and the peasantry of Mexico in general, continued receiving subsidies under the Salinas program. But under Salinas and his successor, Ernesto Zedillo, these subsidies have been gradually reduced as Mexico was integrated into NAFTA and the country's market was thrown open to the importation of cheap corn from the United States. It is no wonder that one of the early communiqués of the EZLN stated that NAFTA "is a death certificate for the Indian peoples of Mexico."

But the most devastating measure taken by the Salinas government against the peasantry was the gutting in 1992 of agrarian reform Article 27 of the Mexican constitution. Owing to peasant agitation in Chiapas over the decades, 54 per cent of the state's land had fallen under the control of *ejidos* or Indian communal associations.[26] While much of this land tended to be the poorest in the state, the changes in Article 27 made it clear that not only would it be impossible for the Indians and peasants to secure access to any more land, but that *ejidos* and communal land holdings would be rolled back. The Salinas "reforms" made it possible to buy and sell these lands, thus opening them up to the vissitudes of the free market and the power of the ascendant capitalist class of large ranchers, plantation owners, and the growing, but small group of enriched peasants and farmers.

Even before the uprising of the EZLN, the conflict in Chiapas had deepened in response to Salinas's neo-liberal modernization policies. In Chiapas, Patrocinio Gonzalez Garrido took office as governor at the same time as Salinas. Faced with a series of land disputes and peasant mobilizations, Gonzalez Garrido first tried to mediate in these disputes, but then turned to repression, aligning himself with the large landowners and the *guardias blancas*. In early 1989, just months after he took office, two of the principal *campesino* leaders in the state were assassinated. During 1990 a protest of small-scale sugar producers was fired upon, leaving six people injured, and several months later peaceful protesters marching on the state capital of Tuxtla Gutierrez were fired upon. During the same period several land settlements that even had presidential decrees in their favor were violently uprooted by state police and landowners.[27]

The conflict in Chiapas moved to the national stage when 400 Indians from Palenque in the rain forest area marched on Mexico City in 1992 after members of the Committee for the Defense of Indian Liberty were arrested, beaten and tortured by the state police while protesting against local corruption, the lack of democracy in municipal government, and the failure of the government to carry out promised public works. The march on the capital touched a national chord of sympathy, coinciding with the changes in Article 27 and a growing awareness of the abysmal living conditions of indigenous peoples throughout Mexico.

Neither Salinas nor Gonzalez Garrido responded to the protesters' demands for change. Indeed, the repression continued and arrest orders were put out for 30 members of the Indian Defense Committee. In Chiapas, the recently formed National Independent Campesino Alliance Emiliano Zapata (ANCIEZ) went underground to become involved in preparations for the armed rebellion that culminated with the uprising of the EZLN on January 1, 1994.[28]

DEMOCRACY AND REBELLION

The rebellion in Chiapas is the product of a quarter of a century of intensive capitalist modernization and a growing resistance by peasant and Indian organizations. It is a rebellion against a government that has nominally proclaimed its commitment to revolutionary reforms and democracy while actually using repression and the free market to consolidate the position of a new ruling class. The Zapatista movement's familiarity with the limits of taking state power in the name of revolution explains why its platform and politics focus on civil society, the demand for authentic democracy, and the transforming of society from the bottom up.

This postmodernist perspective permeates even Indian villages in the rain forest that had no contact with the EZLN before the January 1 uprising. In March 1994, as part of an international delegation that went to Chiapas, I visited the Indian village of Cascada, near Palenque, the site of the magnificent old Mayan ruins. In a meeting with many of the community members, it was striking that the women's organization took the lead in discussing the community's needs and plans as well as the obstacles it faced. They wanted decent schools, medical services, and financial assistance so they could attend nearby technical colleges, as well as the right to elect their own representatives at the municipal and state level. They also wanted lands from the nearby cattle estate to augment the production on their own marginal *ejido*, which the government had granted them back in 1960. But as the ecological representative of the community pointed out, they were fully cognizant of the fact that these lands could only be farmed with appropriate technologies to avoid impoverishing the delicate soils of the region.

One should not fall into the trap of romanticizing the EZLN or the struggle of the indigenous peoples of Chiapas. But the community of Cascada, like hundreds and even thousands of other villages and towns in Chiapas, is in the forefront of the global effort to search for alternative paths of development. The movement in Chiapas has already shaken Mexican society and pushed the country's political discourse to new levels. The movement's success or failure in resisting the onslaught of the global market, mobilizing civil society and stopping government repression and manipulation will be critical in determining the pace of authentic and progressive change that Mexico undergoes in the new century.

9   Zapatismo and the Intergalactic Age

Fiona Jeffries

The Zapatistas gained a tremendous amount of national and global attention when they unexpectedly emerged from the jungle in Mexico's southern state of Chiapas and declared war on neo-liberal globalization. On the day the North American Free Trade Agreement (NAFTA) went into effect, the Zapatista National Liberation Army (EZLN) occupied the old colonial city of San Cristobal de las Casas and four other regional municipalities, emptied prisons, occupied municipal buildings and town centers, commandeered radio stations, spoke to the press and talked to astonished crowds. The militia wore ski masks or scarves around their faces, some carried arms and others had only reasonable facsimiles—sticks carved and painted to look like armaments. "This isn't about Chiapas—it's about NAFTA and Salinas's whole neoliberal project" explained the EZLN's chief spokesperson, Sub-comandante Marcos on the first day of the uprising.[1]

Immediately, news of the rebellion and Zapatista communiqués spread throughout Mexico and around the world. Through their communication practices, the initially local Zapatista army became quickly transformed into a broad national and transnational movement of Zapatismo. The new "local-global" politics of Zapatismo marked a radical departure from that of the globalizing capitalist culture and traditional left internationalism. The Zapatistas communicated a discourse and praxis of revolution unlike any other previous political movement. It challenged not only the neo-liberal world order, but also conventional political wisdom across the spectrum. In Mexico and internationally, a broadly-based civil society movement immediately sprung up around the Zapatistas's demands for democracy and social justice and their critique of neo-liberal globalization. Here we will look at some of the ways in which the emergence of Zapatismo can be seen as a test case of radical democratic communications against global capitalism and for humanity.

From the start, the Zapatistas emphasized the communicational aspect of their struggle. They transformed the conventional militaristic conception of revolution into a political-communicational one. The Zapatistas argued that they had been given no choice but to rise up in arms to demand recognition of their historic place within Mexican society and to bring national and world attention to the dire consequences of globalization. A January 6, 1994, communiqué opens with the following explanation:

> On January 1 of this year, our Zapatista troops began a series of political-military actions whose primary objective was to inform the Mexican people and the rest of the world about the miserable conditions in which millions of Mexicans, especially us, the indigenous people, live and die. With these actions we also let the world know of our decision to fight for our most elementary rights in the only way that the governmental authorities has left us: armed struggle.[2]

Reiterating this in a general way in a communiqué from January 13, the EZLN wrote of the government's military strategy: "They forget that war is not a matter of weapons or large numbers of armed men, but of politics."[3]

FOR A WORLD WHERE MANY WORLDS FIT

The Zapatistas have already accomplished, in spite of enormous odds, much of what they set out to do: they have opened up a space for new kinds of dialogue within Mexico and throughout the world about democracy, justice, pluralism, the organization of power and the culture of power that sustains it. They are challenging the homogenizing thrust of neo-liberal globalization with a reverse global narrative that transcends time and place. By directly confronting the universalist authoritarian traditions associated with capitalist globalization as well as conventional revolutionary politics, the Zapatistas have articulated a radical perspective on revolution and democracy that speaks not for, but of a myriad of excluded experiences.

The Zapatistas provide an important theoretical and experiential critique of globalization. They have done this not just through the use of the electronic media, but also through the politicization of dialogue as a mode of revolutionary practice. An on-going dialogue with local, national and international civil society is central to the Zapatista revolution. By this critical contribution to a radical re-conceptualization of politics at the so-called "End of History," the worldwide phenomenon of Zapatismo can be seen as the other face of the global communications revolution.

The EZLN has sought to make this discourse concrete by sponsoring a variety of meetings with national and international civil society. First in the peace negotiations with the government in the spring of 1994, the EZLN used the opportunity to open a dialogue with civil society and invited hundreds of delegates to come to San Cristobal. Then in the summer of 1994, after the EZLN village assemblies rejected the government's peace proposal, they sponsored the National Democratic Convention where national civil society was invited to come to Zapatista-held territory and hold a dialogue about the future of the popular struggle on a national level. In the spring of 1995 they held a national poll, or consultation, on what the future of the EZLN should be. They set up their own polling networks and over a million people participated. When the dialogue with the government was renewed in April 1995, the EZLN again invited hundreds of activists and advisers to take part.

The year 1996 was an exceptionally busy one as a series of workshops on indigenous rights and culture were held in January 1996 in San Cristobal and another on the reform of the state in July 1996. In April 1996 the EZLN held a Continental Gathering in their territory, inviting activists from throughout the hemisphere to come to discuss the various experiences of neo-liberal restructuring and the fight for democracy in the Americas. Then later in 1996, the EZLN organized the Intercontinental Encounter for Humanity and Against Neo-Liberalism, a meeting with international civil society convened as the beginning of a "local-global" dialogue.

The mass-mediated politics and communicational practices of the EZLN have proven to be central to its very survival. A worldwide dialogue has opened up among a range of movements on the meaning of democracy, liberty and justice in the new world order. Here discourse and praxis are interwoven through the appropriation of a variety of communication media and the elaboration of an alternative social project. Among the actors, both the practice and discourse of radical democracy emphasize several overlapping principles: pluralism, horizontalism, global solidarity, local and popular participation and dialogue. According to the U.S.-based *Accion Zapatista*: "Endless dialogue and the elaboration of a new political culture with non-hierarchical relationships across cultural difference are central to defining, developing, and circulating Zapatismo."[4]

RADICAL DEMOCRACY AND CIVIL SOCIETY

The Zapatistas have consistently argued that they are not a revolutionary vanguard, do not aspire to being a political party and do not hold a blueprint for a future world order. Nor are they seeking to seize state power. Rather, they are calling for a democratic transformation directed by civil society. "We do not want to struggle for power, because the struggle for power is central to the world we reject; it does not form part of the world we want."[5] A stance that violates the norms of conventional political wisdom, the Zapatista position derives from experience and experimentation. The principle of "command obeying" advocated by the Zapatistas is an example of radical democracy in action that also challenges finite conceptualizations of the possible. "Command obeying" is what it says it is: "those who lead should be effectively subjected to the rule of those whom they claim to lead."[6] It means that people are not subjects but actors, and leaders are subject to the determination of leadership through democratic dialogue, local participation and the construction of autonomous systems of decisionmaking.

Their example reveals some possibilities about the relationship between democracy and revolution in the global era. "The essential contribution of the Zapatistas," Patricia King and Francisco Javier Villanueva suggest, "was to demonstrate democracy to those on the Left who preached revolution, and demonstrate revolution to those advocating democracy."[7] Emphasizing a locally constructed praxis of democracy applicable across a range of social contexts, the Zapatista radical democratic project is essentially a re-appropriation of populism from institutional, state and corporate definitions.

Through their communiqués, the Zapatistas have continuously explained the problems of hegemonic structures of power and rule that have led to the present situation, where we find ourselves in an increasingly plutocratic and oligarchic global system. In a letter addressed to national and international civil society, Marcos explains why the Zapatista proposals are subversive (almost) everywhere:

> It is not our arms that make us radical; it is the new political practice which we propose and in which we are immersed with thousands of men and women in Mexico and the world: the construction of a political practice which does not seek the taking of power but the organization of society. Intellectuals, political leadership, of all sizes, of the ultraright, of the right, the center, of

the left and the ultraleft, national and international criticize our proposal. We are so radical that we do not fit in the parameters of "modern political science". We are not bragging madam: we are pointing out the facts. Is there anything more radical than to propose to change the world? You know this because you share this dream with us, and because, though the truth be repeated, we dream it together.[8]

The Zapatistas make constant reference to civil society as an "historical subject." In this framework, the empowerment and self-conscious actions of civil society are seen as engendering new possibilities for a democratic social project in a period apparently marked by the demise of a revolutionary "subject". Here we find a much more genuinely populist left politics where a negative construction of "the masses"—as used by the traditional left—is positively re-cast in the shape of a civil society majority. Their communiqués emphasize an image of civil society that is a web of complex social, political, economic and cultural relationships. The Zapatistas implore us to look at the lies of Power in this new world order and see that radical transformation can be dreamed about only with the participation of an increasingly excluded majority. This is not a utopian vision of a "happy global civil society", but a call to action, to elaborate upon a movement for democratic transformation that is only made possible through the articulation of a multitude of social projects and proposals determined democratically.

Ethically, the Zapatistas themselves act like a mirror for all of us as they expose hidden truths about the twisted image of the modern "global village." Aside from the obvious security considerations, the Zapatistas explain that their trademark balaclavas, or masks, symbolize polar worlds: the faceless global majority excluded from decisionmaking on the one hand, and the disguise of the modernizing state and an increasingly small global ruling class on the other. Several weeks after the new year uprising, Marcos explained the political role of the mask and made a proposition to civil society:

> But when Mexican civil society takes off its own mask it will realize, with much greater impact, that it has been sold an image of itself that is fake, and that the reality is more terrifying than people supposed. If we show each other our faces, the big difference will be that the "Sup-Marcos" always knew what he looked like, while civil society will have to wake up from the long

and lazy dream that "modernity" imposes on everything and everybody. "Sup-Marcos" is ready to take off his ski mask; is Mexican civil society ready to take off its mask?[9]

The ambiguity of the term "civil society" lends itself to both confusion and critical evaluation. Clearly, civil society itself is unevenly organized on the global, national and local levels. It holds a variety of interests, struggles and conceptions of reality. Despite the easy road to the heights of abstraction that an uncritical notion of civil society generates, the radical notion of civil society proposed by the Zapatistas holds the capacity for adaptation and the continuous elaboration of an alternative social project. Harry Cleaver proposes a definition of civil society in the context of Zapatismo: it is "all those moments and movements within society that resist, intentionally or not, subordination to capitalist institutions and, in many cases, fight for alternative ways of organizing society."[10] In an oft-quoted communiqué, Marcos outlines, in a characteristically polemic fashion clearly intended to rattle all conventions, the Zapatista conceptualization of civil society:

Marcos is Gay in San Francisco, a black in South Africa, Asian in Europe, a Chicano in San Isidro, and anarchist in Spain, a Palestinian in Israel, an indigenous person in the streets of San Cristobal, a gang member in Neza, a rocker on Campus, a Jew in Germany, an ombudsman in the Department of Defense, a feminist in a political party, a communist in the post-Cold War period, a prisoner in Cintalapa, a pacifist in Bosnia, a Mapuche in the Andes, a teacher in the National Confederation of Educational Workers, an artist without a gallery or a portfolio, a housewife in any neighborhood in any city in any part of Mexico on a Saturday night, a guerrilla in Mexico at the end of the twentieth century, a striker at the CTM, a sexist in the feminist movement, a woman alone in a Metro station at 10 p.m., a retired person standing around in the Zocalo, a peasant without land, an underground editor, an unemployed worker, a doctor with no office, a nonconformist student, a dissident against neoliberalism, a writer without books or readers and a Zapatista in the Mexican southeast. In other words, Marcos is a human being in this world. Marcos is every untolerated, oppressed, exploited minority that is resisting and saying "Enough."[11]

LIBERTY, JUSTICE AND DEMOCRACY

The Zapatistas' re-conceptualization of three traditional revolution-ary ideals—social justice, democracy and liberty—have come to be widely debated in Mexico and beyond by those trying to articulate a radical politics relevant to the present situation. Just as the Zapatistas form a critical node in the articulation of a de-centered debate on the left about capitalist and revolutionary universalism, their interpretation of liberty, justice and democracy emerges from the margins of power, from locally constructed and centuries old praxis of resistance to the homogenizing impulse of imperial, national and global integration.

The notions of liberty, justice and democracy appear to be totally appropriated by the discourse of globalization and free markets—liberty means the liberty to shop with abandon, democracy means the "democratic free market;" and justice is confused with the "justice" of policing, punishment and the penal system. June Nash notes the relevance of the Zapatistas' alternative interpretation of these principles: "*Justice* means not to punish, but to give back to each what he or she deserves, and that is what the mirror gives back." *Liberty* is "not that each one does what he or she wants, but to choose whatever road that the mirror wants in order to arrive at the true word." *Democracy* requires "not that all think the same, but that all thoughts or the majority of the thoughts seek and arrive at a good agreement." [12]

In a communiqué addressed to several national publications 20 days after the uprising, Marcos explains how the Zapatista conception of these principles is divergent from conventional vanguard movements:

We think that revolutionary change in Mexico is not just a question of one kind of activity. It will come, strictly speaking, from neither an armed revolution nor an unarmed one. It will be the result of struggles on several fronts, using a lot of methods, various social forms, with different levels of commitment and par-ticipation. And the result will not be the triumph of a party, organization, or alliance of organizations with their particular social programs, but rather the creation of a democratic space for resolving the confrontations between different political proposals. This democratic space will have three fundamental premises that are historically inseparable: the democratic right of determining the dominant social project, the freedom to subscribe to one project or another, and the requirement that all projects must point the way to justice.[13]

This conception brings up some important questions regarding the relationship between the local and the global and the meaning of another standard revolutionary ideal: solidarity. In practice, the concept of solidarity has often been distorted by the deeply unequal global distribution of wealth and power. The Zapatista view of solidarity is not a unilateral relationship that reflects and reinforces the paternalistic gaze from the "first world" to the "third world." Nor is it about solidarity among a few insiders (national, organizational or ideological). Nor is it a distant solidarity among cosmopolitan "global" activists and professionals found at official "global meetings" like the UN-sponsored Rio and Beijing summits. In the Zapatista mirror, solidarity is the building of alternative resistance networks around the world through the practice of radical democracy, liberty and social justice with a related emphasis on localism, autonomy and horizontal relationships among all the participating groups and organizations.

CREATING ALTERNATIVE GLOBAL NETWORKS OF RESISTANCE

The Zapatista principles of democracy and horizontalism are highly applicable to the more general project of democratic communication networks. The creation of horizontal networks versus the establishment of a centralized mass organization takes advantage of the process of globalization and the information revolution. In the praxis of Zapatismo, the struggle against neo-liberalism is necessarily a global one and the struggle for humanity demands an ethic of democracy.

Over the last decade electronic networks have proliferated around the world. Business and governments have touted the use of the Internet as the way to boost profits and work out more effective and efficient forms of social control in the era of globalization. On the other side, the network concept is also being promoted as an effective and more democratic mode of organizing against globalization. Such networks are more like a reflection of civil society itself—a vast complex array of groups and individuals working in diverse political, cultural and economic contexts, with particular programs and ideas. These networks are used to circulate articles, analyses and urgent actions on a variety of issues, from a diversity of sources (mainstream press, isolated communities, alternative media, NGOs), located in various locales (from Mexico to Argentina, Spain to India, the U.S. to Nigeria).

The anti-NAFTA coalition networks were an historic lesson in the process of building a theory and practice of transnational organizing. If NAFTA was the first and most sweeping free trade agreement of the neo-liberal era, opposition to it was the first to use the new communications media to create a sweeping transnational dialogue among a variety of groups. Environmental, indigenous, women and labor groups were some of the major movers in the anti-NAFTA campaigns in Canada, the United States and Mexico. Having brought a wide cross-section of continental civil society into the debate about globalization, the infrastructure for a massive response to the uprising in Chiapas was already in place the day that NAFTA became law. Initially, after the uprising, national and international civil society used the networks established throughout the anti-NAFTA campaigns to avert a full-scale military response from the Mexican government.

But it soon erupted into a vast transnational network. Neither the Zapatistas nor those expressing solidarity with them were dependent solely upon reports issued by journalists working for mainstream outlets. Critical reports coming out of Chiapas, especially those from various NGOs and independent journalists, spread rapidly throughout Mexico and the world, linking up diverse movements to the Zapatistas.

The Zapatista networks continue to function across the world. The intent is several-fold as various groups interact not only to express their solidarity with the Zapatistas, but also to address specific local issues. Discussions and the formulation of strategies takes place transnationally, informing network participants about events, actions and campaigns taking place in various locales. Groups also share information and analysis on a wide range of issues, while synthesizing and re-publishing articles and information from magazines, newspapers and so on. This information-sharing encompasses issues and groups not directly related to the Zapatista movement, serving instead a broader movement which counters neo-liberalism as a global phenomenon.

At the moment, there are hundreds of groups working in this manner around the globe. For example, the People's Global Action

(PGA) network emerged out of Europe following the two Zapatista-inspired Intercontinental meetings and appears to represent a kind of organizing unique to the global informational period. Not an organization, but a network of local movements stretched throughout various parts of the world, the PGA is a horizontal network capable of coordinating actions which target the global policy apparatus. Thus, in May and June of 1999 the participating groups, which range from a large agrarian union in India to an urban environmentalist organization in London, converged in Geneva and other European centers to protest against the annual meeting of the G-7 executive. The PGA also sponsored and participated in gatherings at the headquarters of the World Bank and campaigns targeting various transnational corporations, such as Monsanto. Much of this type of networking allows for more spontaneous, less hierarchical and more open forms of organization.

THE INTERGALACTIC ENCOUNTER AND THE NEO-ZAPATISTA INTERNATIONAL OF HOPE

These modes of communication, particularly the Internet, played a key role in organizing the Zapatista-sponsored Intergalactic *encuentro*, or encounter, in 1996. Two and a half years after the January uprising, the Zapatistas drew thousands of activists, intellectuals and media outlets to the Lacandona jungle. The "First Intergalactic Encounter for Humanity and Against Neo-Liberalism," convened in five Zapatista communities, was a remarkable event that demonstrated the creativity and expansive vision of the Zapatistas and their civilian bases of support. The title given to the first intercontinental gathering sponsored by the EZLN in 1996 reflected a transnational attempt to articulate a broad politics of "No against neo-liberalism and yes for humanity." The intent was to create a local and international pluralist politics by networking movements with common and distinct projects and proposals.

The invitation to the Encounter was issued in January 1996 with the "Declaration of La Realidad." In this document the EZLN outlined the goal of establishing a new international—an International of Hope. The Intergalactica represented the search for a different kind of politics in relation to the present conditions and, according to Holloway and Pelaez, "demonstrated clearly that the Zapatistas' struggle was not just a local one, nor an ethnic, nor a national one, but a struggle understood as the struggle of humanity for humanity."[14] The overarching theme of the Encounter was the development of a new, de-centralized and horizontal international-ism structured around a transnational network of movements. It would be the opposite face (or mask) of globalism—the face of resistance to the centripetal impulse of transnational capitalism. The EZLN called for the establishment of genuine forms of solidarity based on common struggles and respect for locally determined proposals. Not an international of charity, or bureaucratic centralism, but a horizontally organized counter-globalism from below. The invitation in poetic prose, called for:

> The international of hope. Not the bureaucracy of hope, not the opposite image and, thus, the same as that which annihilates us. Not the Power with a new sign or new clothing. A breath like this, the breath of dignity. A flower yes, the flower of hope. A song yes, the song of life.[15]

Over 3,000 people from 43 countries were hosted in five Zapatista communities. The general gathering was called *Aguascalientes*, in reference to a similar assembly of Mexican revolutionaries over eight decades earlier.[16] Feminists, indigenous activists, environmentalists, union activists, academics, media workers, members of urban and rural organizations, liberation theologists, gay, lesbian and human rights activists, students, artists, Anarchists, Marxists, youth contin-gents, cyberpunks and many others, with various and overlapping movement affiliations, attended the gathering. Five general "worktables," each with several sub-themes were designated for discussion and the formulation of strategy. The initial themes had been worked out several months earlier at the "Continental Encounter" that brought together activists from around the Americas, and fell into six broad categories: Politics, Economics, Society, Culture, Identity and Diversity.

The themes shifted again once participants arrived and debated the content to be explored over the next five days in their various tables. The substance of the topics decided upon is found in the post-Encounter publication, *Cronicas Intergalacticas* (Intergalactic Chronicles). The thematic headings were: "What is the Politics We Have, and What Politics Do We Need?" "The Economic Question: Horror Stories," "All Cultures For Everyone, and The Media? From Graffiti to Cyberspace," "What Society is Not Civil?" and "In This

World, Many Worlds Fit." As demonstrated in the titles, each group addressed two general and interwoven themes: the nature of the neo-liberal world order in local and global contexts and the sources of collective strength at the grassroots of global civil society.

Following the opening plenary participants were scattered throughout the five *Aguascalientes* communities to hold discussions and formulate strategies around the themes. Three days later participants convened again at La Realidad where the substance of the smaller group debates and proposals for action were shared. The proposals were both grand and numerous, metaphysical and concrete, but there was a general coherence that emphasized some basic principles: 1. Zapatismo is a movement in constant transformation, always subject to new elaborations; 2. the creation of alternative social, political, economic and cultural structures is integral to combating the destructive impulse of global capitalism; 3. the need to create horizontal and multilayered local, national, regional and intercontinental networks against neo-liberalism and for humanity; 4. the recognition and celebration of the complexity of social reality that avoids the pitfalls of reductionism; 5. the oppressive traditions of sexism and racism need to be confronted in all aspects of struggle and solidarity; and 6. neither the earth nor human cultures are objects up for sale. A key thread running through each of the sets of general proposals was the centrality of liberating the media from corporate and state monopolies in order to create a democratic communications infrastructure.

At the closing plenary in La Realidad the EZLN emphasized that the best way to support the Zapatistas is to struggle against neo-liberalism as a global phenomenon while fighting for humanity with concrete local projects based on genuine forms of social solidarity. They argued that the Encounter reflected something much deeper and wider than the bodies and ideas circulating around the five *Aguascalientes* meetings. In his closing speech Marcos explained that history is still very much alive, that the meetings represented a radical counter to the neo-liberal contention that all social projects are moribund and irrelevant:

> To whom does it matter how and what we dream here or in any part of the world? Who are they who dare to convene with their dream all the dreams of the world? What's happening in the mountains of the Mexican Southeast that finds echo and mirror in the streets of Europe, suburbs of Asia, rural areas of America,

townships of Africa and houses of Oceania? What's happening with the peoples of these five continents that, so we are told, only encountered each other to make war or compete? Wasn't this turn of the century synonymous with despair, bitterness, and cynicism? From where and how did all these dreams arrive at reality?[17]

Thus, the explicit goal of the Encounter was to go beyond the dialogical and put a concrete face on the call for an International of Hope. While the face-to-face dialogue would continue with a second Intercontinental meeting scheduled—in a symbolic reversal of history—for the following summer in Spain, the intervening and long-term assignment was the establishment of a worldwide network of resistance:

A network of voices that resist the war that the Power wages on them. A network of voices that not only speak, but also struggle and resist for humanity and against neoliberalism. A network of voices that are born resisting, reproducing their resistance in other even quieter or lonelier voices. A network that covers the five continents and helps to resist the death that the Power promises.[18]

CRACKS IN THE MIRROR AND MULTIMEDIA SUBVERSIVES

"What governments should really fear is an expert in communications technology"—Marcos.

There is a common misconception that the Zapatista army is up in the jungle logging onto the Internet and directly sending communiqués around the world, when in fact the EZLN is involved in horizontal networking with actual living people scattered around the globe. This misunderstanding points to a very important issue in regards to the new communicational politics: the Internet is an adaptable, incremental and potentially communal tool despite the fact that corporate and institutional interests dominate it. If the new articulation of capitalist hegemony is built upon a global-informational paradigm, then radical democratic movements seeking to build an alternative local and global order are faced with the necessity of organizing transnationally by using the same tools of communication upon which global capital relies. Overall, the establishment of the networks of communication are occurring both virtually and materially as groups interact through various communication media globally as well as by making face to face contact in particular locations. These networks are operating horizontally across the globe to subvert globalization itself, whether it is by coordinating job action by workers on the U.S.–Mexico border, organizing counter-meetings to the G-7, or sending video equipment and trainers into the Lacandona jungle.

The vast majority of the world's computers, telephone lines, newspaper output, and information technologies are located in the North. Fifty per cent of the world's computers are in the U.S., while the majority of users within North America continue to be predominantly white, male middle-class professionals.[19] Furthermore, this new information and communication order is not necessarily open and horizontal since hierarchies are built into the technological paradigm. Owing to the tremendous amount of material available on the Internet, information sifters are generally required to decide upon the relevant material to be posted or distributed. Thus, issues such as whose stories get told and shared, and who gets what information for what purposes are inextricable from the existing inequalities of access to information, resources and power. Given the increasing relevance of information and communication technologies in structuring relationships of power, the existence of information itself clearly does not mechanically create the conditions for democracy or social justice.

The fact that the technologies are developed largely for military-industrial-financial purposes immediately make them suspect. The structural emphasis on individualism that accompanies the computer form, as well as the problems of access and the exclusivity associated with computers, creates hierarchies within groups and divisions between those linked and those not linked. These are some of the limitations of the new media. Cleaver argues that while many alternative social movements ally themselves across borders through the various communication networks, there is tremendous concern on the part of the commercial and military sectors about how to stem the flow of non-commercial and alternative interactions.[20]

The issue of appropriation is key here since it is not merely the existence of "technology" that brings new possibilities for democratic communication, but rather what is being created with that technology by oppositional groups around the world. These groups are the opposite face of the "information revolution" as they consciously work towards creating a new communicational commons that simultaneously links and transcends time and space. Zapatismo is a test-case example of how the appropriation of informational tools for the elaboration of alternative social projects can have remarkable concrete effects.

In this context, new information technologies are not deployed as the primary political tool by oppositional movements. Rather, they are treated politically, as complementary tools that must be appropriated in a social sense. This means emphasizing collective rather than individual involvement. Cleaver calls the Zapatista-style appropriation of new information technologies "the electronic fabric of struggle."[21] This new mode of (inter)action has transformed the relationship between senders and receivers as the capacity for interaction and dialogue has expanded. More and more, receivers are also senders, and as shown with the Zapatistas, actors are also authors. These networks are potentially vast and have contributed to a reverse global narrative from below. This has led to what Lins Ribiero calls, "the technosymbolic basis" of supporting the emergence of a "virtual imagined transnational community.[22] In a series compiled by U.S.-based *Accion Zapatista*, the relevance of cyberspace for radical organizing is outlined as follows:

> Computers have also made possible a new kind of organizing very much in keeping with the spirit of Zapatista organizing in Chiapas. Computer networks allow the creation of a rapid and free flowing fabric of democratic communication and cooperation. Unlike traditional organizations, which have tended to have rigid, top-down hierarchical structures—including revolutionary organizations—this electronic fabric of organization is a horizontal networking with infinite cross-linking. Efforts to IMPOSE hierarchical structures in cyberspace are very difficult because participants can easily abandon such a terrain and create their own contacts, lists, conferences or newsgroups.[23]

A central issue is whether the information technologies are in the service of movements or whether movements are relegated to the technological imperative. Is it all an intellectual fantasy of dreamy global activists to appropriate these new technologies? Too academic? Too abstract? In dealing with these questions, we should not allow ourselves to fall into technological determinism. Technology is always a social and political construct that is organized and applied by people. Among other contributions to a new revolutionary politics, Zapatismo has helped us understand that the information age can be turned to our advantage only if we take the initiative in shaping the new technologies for a new humanity and against corporate-driven globalization.

Epilogue
The Millennial Cracks

With the advent of the new millennium, popular resistance to globalization has intensified as the global elites scurry to prop up the institutions that sustain their prerogatives. The massive demonstrations against the World Bank and the International Monetary Fund in Washington D.C. in April 2000 marked yet another milestone in the rebellion against global neo-liberalism that began with the Zapatista uprising in 1994. The protests of French workers and farmers in the mid-to-late 1990s, the strikes and uprisings in Indonesia and South Korea in 1997 and 1998 due to the Asian financial crisis, and the more recent revolts in early 2000 of Ecuadorian Indians and Bolivians against neo-liberal austerity policies—these very diverse protests and uprisings make it clear that a vibrant global movement is determined to reverse the plundering of the planet by the world's dominant financial and corporate interests.

The protests in Washington D.C. showed conclusively that the demonstrations four and a half months earlier in Seattle against the World Trade Organization were no fluke. The international movement against corporate-driven globalization has put down deep roots, even in the world's most powerful nation. A commentary in *Business Week* on the Washington demonstrations declared: "this cause won't easily disappear ... this radical but committed movement could really have an impact..."[1]

Particularly noteworthy in Washington was the participation of youth. If the Battle of Seattle introduced a new politics of protest to the United States, the demonstrations in Washington marked the unequivocal appearance of a new generation of activists dedicated to challenging globalization and the powerful financial and corporate institutions that stand behind it. As the *Washington Post* noted: "most of the demonstrators were young."[2] They came in chartered buses, cars, planes and trains, predominantly from east coast cities, but also from California, Oregon, Washington State and many points in between.

The anti-sweatshop campaign, which is particularly strong on U.S. university campuses, fed into this insurgent youth movement. At many universities across the U.S., workshops and meetings were held to prepare for the new battle in Washington. Just a week before the protests, a conference was organized at New York University called: "Labor's next century: alliances, sweatshops and the global South." Hundreds of students attended two days of workshops, discussing issues such as the political economy of globalization and campaigns against corporations such as Nike for their third world labor policies. Direct Action, one of the main organizations involved in civil disobedience in Seattle and Washington, was also present at the conference, discussing tactics and strategies.

The young anarchists, who created such a stir in Seattle, swelled their ranks from about 50 in Seattle to upwards of 300 in Washington. They called themselves the "Black Bloc," referring to their black garb and flags as well as their official name, the Revolutionary Anti-Capitalist Bloc. They were the more combative contingent of the youth movement. While they paraded through Washington chanting "Whose streets? Our streets," the anarchists focused their more strident actions on trying to breach the metal and armed police barriers preventing access to the World Bank and the IMF. They also threw up their own barricades comprised of newspaper boxes, chain-link fencing and whatever else they could scavenge from the streets to block the police from attacking them and other protesters.

In Seattle the demonstrators were successful in disrupting the meetings of the World Trade Organization on its first day. In Washington, the demonstrators could claim no such victory as the two days of scheduled meetings of the World Bank and the IMF on April 16 and 17 went off punctually. The Japanese delegation arrived at four in the morning on the first day to avoid the demonstrators, while many other delegations assembled at designated hotels to be taken to the meetings in vans and buses with armed police escorts that pierced the lines of protesters blocking World Bank and IMF entrances.

But the punctual meetings of the world's leading lending institutions were a Pyrrhic victory. Like the WTO meetings in Seattle, the "whole world was watching" due to the demonstrators. As the *Business Week* commentary noted: "The protesters don't want respect—they want attention and they got it. They scored a big win ... dominating the news, holding down page one of every major newspaper."[3] In scenes reminiscent of the anti-war protests of the 1960s, newspapers from New York to London to New Delhi carried front page photos of police clubbing demonstrators as they marched and chanted slogans like "dump the fund," "break the bank," and "more world, less bank," referring to the IMF and the World Bank.

CRACKS AMONG THE ELITES

Even before the demonstrations in Washington, members of the global elite were questioning the role and mission of the world's top financial institutions. Joseph Stiglitz, the chief economist of the World Bank until November 1999, wrote a scathing critique of the policies of the IMF in *The New Republic*. He declared that the protesters coming to Washington were essentially right in their charges that "the IMF is arrogant," that it "doesn't really listen to the developing countries," that it "is secretive and insulated from democratic accountability," and, finally, that "the IMF's economic 'remedies' often make things worse." Perhaps his most poignant statement was: "The older men who staff the fund—and they are overwhelmingly older men—act as if they are shouldering Rudyard Kipling's white man's burden."[4]

Stiglitz, however, like most members of the elite, supports the existent global order, believing that if only a few executives at the top are changed and adjustments are made in the IMF's policies, the process of globalization will proceed unimpeded. He, for example, argued that in Latin America, unlike Asia, the IMF has generally got it right with "fiscal austerity (balanced budgets) and tighter monetary policies." Stiglitz said nothing about the forced privatization of public sector enterprises that has enabled private capital, particularly transnational corporations, to rip off enormous profits by taking over water, electric and telephone utilities while gobbling up lucrative state-owned petroleum and mining enterprises.

Stiglitz's critique was in effect a post mortem assessment. The chief "old man" he criticized at the IMF, Michel Camdessus, had already resigned as head of the IMF in December 1999. The new director, Horst Kohler, appointed after much bickering among the G-7 nations, made it clear that he would assemble a new staff and strive to avoid the policy failures of southeast Asia and Russia.

These token changes at the top were little more than feeble attempts to temper the growing storm from below against corporate-driven globalization. While the demonstrators marched on the streets of Washington in mid-April, the Group of 77, an organization representing the governments of 80 per cent of the world's population, met in Havana, Cuba, at a conference that was attended by over 40 heads of state. The prime minister of Belize, Said Musa, reflected the prevailing sentiment at the conference, declaring that economic policies dictated by the dominant countries had not stabilized economies, but had instead "stabilized poverty." Added South African President Thabo Mbeki: "We believe consciousness is rising, including in the north about the inequality and insecurity globalization has brought."[5]

Stiglitz was part of an emergent new consensus, or "Third Way," that called for reshaping the mandate of the IMF, the World Bank and the World Trade Organization so they can better serve the needs of the dominant interests that stand behind globalization. The strict neo-liberal agenda that drove the policies of these institutions and the globalization process in the 1980s and 1990s was no longer appropriate to the needs of the twenty-first century. By the beginning of 2000 it was widely accepted that the global financial institutions had failed miserably in their effort to manage the crisis in southeast Asia in 1997–98, making a bad situation even worse by imposing austerity policies that restricted mass consumption at a time when the economies of the region needed to be reinflated.

Bill Clinton headed up the call for the Third Way. In his address in Seattle to the WTO, Clinton tried to build a stronger social base for globalization by promoting the inclusion of labor and environmental clauses in any new WTO accords. The Third Way was also endorsed by Clinton's principal cohorts, Tony Blair of Great Britain and Gerhard Schroeder of Germany.

The Third Way is not a return to Keynesian economics. Rather, it upholds the basic neo-liberal tenants of an open global economy and the complete mobility of transnational capital. The state will not usurp the role of private capital, but instead limit itself to providing stable market conditions and the development of "human capital." Orthodox neo-liberalism is modified only to the extent that institutions such as the World Bank are to invest more in education and even health care so that a new workforce is better prepared to become part of the "flexible" labor market.

James Wolfensohn, president of the World Bank, is in the forefront of those adopting the rhetoric of the Third Way. President of the Bank since 1994, Wolfensohn, in a major public address in Thailand in February 2000, acknowledged that the bank had done little to lower global impoverishment. From 1987 to 1998 the number of people living in dire poverty—defined as less than a dollar a day, "remained roughly constant, at about 1.2 billion. Excluding China, the number has actually risen from just under 880 million to over 980 million. In addition, the total number of people living on under $2 a day is now estimated at nearly 3 billion, approaching half the world's population."[6]

Wolfensohn's statistics, while appalling, did not begin to reflect the real impoverishment that has struck the world's population with globalization. *Time* magazine, hardly noted for its anti-globalization leanings, wrote that while the IMF and the World Bank insisted that "their policies will boost living standards over the long term .... people in the Global South have lost patience with such talk." *Time* looked at Tanzania as an example, a country labeled a success story by the IMF and the World Bank as they forced the Tanzanian government to abandon state socialist policies, privatize large sectors of the economy and expand exports to the world market.

James Adams, the World Bank director for Tanzania, declared: "Tanzania has made great progress in getting its macroeconomic situation in order." Adams also claimed that while 65 per cent of Tanzania's population lived in dire poverty in the mid-1980s, that figure had been reduced to 51 per cent. *Time*, however, pointed out that "Tanzanian analysts laugh bitterly" at these statistics. Most of those who live at or near poverty levels are "men and women, almost all subsistence or small-plot cash-crop farmers [who] have been structurally adjusted half to death." Adams omitted "the fact that everything in a farmer's life costs more today," thanks to imposed currency devaluations and the doubling and even quadrupling of prices paid for agricultural inputs such as fertilizers.[7]

It should not be surprising that Wolfensohn, a former senior partner in Wall Street's Salomon Brothers, would view the alleviation of poverty as a "development enterprise." Analogous to Kipling's musings on the "white man's burden," the logic of modernity in the twenty-first century leads inevitably to the belief that highly paid international bureaucrats are destined to fly around the globe dispensing their wisdom on how to uplift the world's poor.

The future lies not with these imperial agents of modernization, but with those in rebellion against the process of globalization, be they Zapatistas, Ecuadorian Indians, French peasants, Asian trade unionists or U.S. environmentalists and anarchists. They are intent on taking control of their own destinies, becoming the new stewards of the planet by creating "one world with room for many worlds."

Notes

INTRODUCTION

1. Al Krebs, "The Calamity Howler," *The Progressive Populist*, January 1–15, 2000.
2. William Greider, "Global Agenda: After the WTO Protest in Seattle, It's Time to Go on the Offensive. Here's How," *The Nation*, January 31, 2000.
3. For an earlier discussion of revolutionary movements and their challenge to the United States, see Roger Burbach, "The Conflict at Home and Abroad: U.S. Imperialism vs the New Revolutionary Societies, in Richard Fagen, Carmen Diana Deere and Jose Luis Coraggio (eds), *Monthly Review Press*, New York, 1986.
4. "Latin America's Economic Reforms," *The Economist*, October 19, 1991.
5. *New York Times*, October 27, 1999.
6. Ibid.
7. Donald Sassoon, *One Hundred Years of Socialism: The West European Left in the Twentieth Century*, The New Press, New York, 1996, pp. 744–46.
8. "Overview," *United Nations Development Report*, UN Publications, New York, 1999.
9. *The Seattle Times*, December 1, 1999, p. 13.
10. Sassoon, "One Hundred Years."
11. John Gray, *False Dawn: The Delusions of Global Capitalism*, The New Press, New York, 1998, p. 21.
12. Ibid., p. 235.
13. Roger Burbach, "Roots of the Postmodern Rebellion in Chiapas," *New Left Review*, No. 205, May–June, 1994.
14. Roger Burbach, Orlando Nunez and Boris Kagarlitsky, *Globalization and Its Discontents: The Rise of Postmodern Socialisms*, Pluto Press, New York & London, 1997.
15. Roger Burbach, "The (Un)defining of Postmodern Marxism: On Narrating New Social and Economic Actors," *Rethinking Marxism*, Spring, 1998.
16. Roger Burbach and William I. Robinson, "The Fin de Siecle Debate: Globalization as Epochal Shift," *Science and Society*, Fall, 1998.
17. Roger Burbach, "Socialism is Dead, Long Live Socialism," NACLA *Report on the Americas*, November–December, 1997.
18. Kevin Danaher and Roger Burbach, *Globalize This! The Battle Against the World Trade Organization and Corporate Rule*, Common Courage Press, Monroe, Maine, 2000.

CHAPTER 1

1. *The Economist* ran a series of articles in October and November 1997 on the debate as seen from capital's perspective while *Business Week* ran an

important article on "The New Economy" on November 17, 1997. For some of the debate on the left, see Linda Weiss, "Globalization and the Myth of the Powerless State," *New Left Review*, September–October, 1997, and the slew of articles and exchanges that appeared in journals such as *Monthly Review, Radical Philosophy, Race and Class, The Nation, Rethinking Marxism*, and elsewhere.

2. Eric Hobsbawm, *The Age of Revolution*, Mentor, New York, 1962; *The Age of Capital*, Sphere, London, 1977; *The Age of Empire*, Pantheon, New York,1987.

3. Eric Hobsbawm, *The Age of Extremes*, Vintage, New York, 1994.

4. *Monthly Review* has taken the lead in staking out this position. See A. Sivanandan and Ellen Meiksins Wood, "Globalization and Epochal Shifts: An Exchange," *Monthly Review*, 48(9): 1997, pp. 19–32. See also Paul Sweezy, "More (or Less) on Globalization," *Monthly Review*, 49(4) 1997, pp. 1–4.

5. Sivanandan and Wood, p. 21.

6. Jorge Castaneda, *Utopia Unarmed*, Vintage, New York, 1993, p. 432.

7. Rudolf Hilferding, *Finance Capital: A Study of the Latest Phase of Capitalist Development*, Routledge, Boston & London, 1981.

8. See William I. Robinson, *Promoting Polyarchy: Globalization, U.S. Intervention, and Hegemony*, Cambridge University Press, Cambridge, 1996. See also Robinson, "Globalisation: Nine Theses of Our Epoch," *Race and Class*, 38(2):1996, pp. 13–31.

9. United Nations Conference on Trade and Development (UNCTAD), *World Investment Report: Investment, Trade and International Policy Arrangements*, United Nations, New York and Geneva, 1996, p. 3.

10. UNCTAD, *World Investment Report: Transnational Corporations, Market Structure and Competition Policy*, United Nations, New York and Geneva 1997, pp. xv–xvi. See also United Nations, Department of Economic and Social Information and Policy Analysis, *World Economic and Social Survey*, United Nations, New York and Geneva, 1997.

11. UNCTAD, 1997, p. xvi.

12. Ibid., p. 44.

13. UNCTAD, 1996, p. 12.

14. Ibid., p. 41.

15. For example, summarizing much of the literature in this regard, Weiss discusses this concentration but does not examine recent variation and historic context. See Weiss, "Globalization," pp. 3–27.

16. For detailed discussion, see Robinson, "Promoting Polyarchy."

17. International Labor Organization (ILO), *World Employment Report 1996–97*, United Nations, Geneva, 1997, p. 2.

18. UNCTAD, 1997, p. xxi.

19. Ibid., p. xvii.

20. UNCTAD, 1996, p. xxxi.

21. Haluk Akdogan, *The Integration of International Capital Markets: Theory and Empirical Evidence*, Edward Elgar, Vermont, 1995, p. 9.

22. World Bank, *Global Economic Prospects and the Developing Countries*, World Bank, Washington, D.C., 1992, p. 33.

23. "One World?," *The Economist*, October 18, 1997, pp. 79–80.

24. *New York Times*, September 20, 1995.
25. Rubi Dornbusch, "Mexico Learned Its Lesson. Now, Will East Asia?", *Business Week*, October 13, 1997, p. 18.
26. "Psst! Want a Nice Pice of a Chaebol," *Business Week*, May 18, 1998, pp. 50–51.
27. "Fast, Cheap, and Ahead of the Pack, *Business Week*, April 5, 1999, p. 36.
28. "One World"?, *The Economist*, October 18, 1997, p. 80.
29. For an important discussion on this point, and for the issues raised in this sub-section, see Leslie Sklair, *Sociology of the Global System* (second revised edition), Johns Hopkins, Baltimore, 1995, esp. Chapter 1. See also William I. Robinson "Maldevelopment in Central America: Globalization and Social Change," *Development and Change* 29(3), 1998, pp. 467–97.
30. See Richaard D. Du Boff, Edward S. Herman, William K. Tabb, Ellen Meiksins Wood, "Debate on Globalization," *Monthly Review*, 49(6), 1997, p. 32. Tabb and Wood argue this position.
31. Philip Mattera, *World Class Business: A Guide to the 100 Most Powerful Global Corporations*, Henry Holt, New York, 1992.
32. Peter Dicken, *Global Shift: The Internationalization of Economic Activity*, Guilford Press, New York: 1992, p. 291.
33. Lorraine Eden and Maureen Appel Molot, 1993, "Insiders and outsiders: defining 'who is us' in the North American automobile industry," in *Transnational Corporations* 2(3), UNCTAD, United Nations, New York and Geneva, 1993, pp. 31–64.
34. See Dicken, "Global Shift", p. 272, calculated on the basis of Figure 9.3.

CHAPTER 2

1. Michel Chossudovsky, *The Globalisation of Poverty: Impacts of IMF and World Bank Reforms*, Zed Books, London and NJ, 1997, and Third World Network, Penang, Malaysia, 1997, p. 26.
2. Ibid., p. 3.
3. Hans-Peter Martin and Harald Schumann, *The Global Trap: Globalization and the Assault on Prosperity and Democracy*, Zed Books, London & New York, 1997, p. 7.
4. William I. Robinson, "Globalisation: Nine Theses of Our Epoch," *Race and Class*, 38(2), 1996, pp. 13–31. See also Robinson, "Maldevelopment in Central America: Globalization and Social Change," *Development and Change* 29(3) 1998, pp. 467–97.
5. United Nations Development Program, *United Nations Human Development Report* 1998, United Nations, New York, 1998.
6. Ibid.
7. Economic Policy Institute and the Center on Budget and Policy Priorities, *Pulling Apart*, Washington D.C., January 2000.
8. *New York Times*, January 19, 2000, p. A21.
9. Carlos Marichal, "Latin America in the Age of the Billionaires," in NACLA *Report on the Americas*, May–June, 1997, pp. 29–31.
10. *New York Times*, January 25, 2000.

11. Alvaro Calderon, Michael Mortimore and Wilson Peres, "Mexico: Foreign Investment as a Source of International Competitiveness," in John H. Dunning and Rafneesh Narula (eds) *Foreign Direct Investment and Governments*, Routledge, New York & London, 1996, pp. 273–74.
12. Marichal, NACLA *Report*, p. 19.
13. Robert Reich on National Public Radio, January 20, 2000.
14. See Chapters 1 and 3 for a discussion of these types of investments.
15. Manuel Castells, "The Power of Identity," in *The Information Age*, Vol. 2, Blackwell, Cambridge, MA, p. 244.
16. Linda Weiss, *The Myth of the Powerless State*, Cornell University Press, Ithaca, New York, 1998, p. 194.
17. Ibid., p. 194.
18. Ibid., p. 209.
19. There is almost a universal conflation of states with nation states in much of the literature on globalization. Global capitalism cannot function without the state. But there is no reason, historically or theoretically, to assume that states are coterminous with nation states.
20. Giovanni Arrighi, *The Long Twentieth Century: Money, Power, and the Origins of Our Times*, Verso, London, 1994.
21. See William I. Robinson, "Globalisation: Nine Theses of Our Epoch," *Race and Class*, 38(2), p. 31.

CHAPTER 3

1. Manuel Castells, *The Information Age*, Vols 1–3, Blackwell Publishers, Cambridge, MA, 1996–98. See also Alvin Toffler, *Powershift: Knowledge, Wealth, and Violence at the Edge of the 21st Century*, Bantam Books, New York, 1991.
2. "A Tale of Two Economies," *Fortune*, April 26, 1999.
3. Matthew Josephson, *The Robber Barons: The Great American Capitalists, 1861–1901*, Harcourt, Brace & Co., New York, 1934, p. vii.
4. "John Malone: Weaving a New Web", *Business Week*, April 19, 1999.
5. "CBS: Can CEO Mel Karmazin Reinvent Network TV?, *Business Week*, April 5, 1999.
6. Ibid.
7. "Bill Gates, Richest American Ever," *Fortune*, August 4, 1997.
8. "Is Greed Good?," *Business Week*, April 19, 1999.
9. Cited in David Bacon, "The New Face of Union Busting," January 13, 1996, Email story. For copy email: dbacon@igc.org.
10. Lenny Siegel, ed. *Global Electronics*, No. 124, Pacific Studies Center, Mountain View, CA. February 1994.
11. Chris Benner, *Growing Together or Drifting Apart, A Status Report on Social and Economic Well-Being in Silicon Valley*, a joint publication of Working Partnerships USA and the Economic Policy Institute, January, 1998, Executive Summary, p. 2.
12. Ibid.
13. Bacon, *The New Face of Union Busting*.
14. Brenner, *Growing Together*, p. 32.

15. *Oakland Tribune*, April 6, 1999, NEWS p. 3.
16. *New York Times*, March 25, 1999.
17. *New York Times*, April 14, 1999.
18. Daniel Burstein and David Kline, *Road Warriors: Dreams and Nightmares Along the Information Highway*, Dutton Press, New York, 1995, p. 336.
19. *New York Times*, May 4, 1999.
20. "Wage Growth Fails to Meet Expectations," *New York Times*, April 30, 1999.
21. Cited in Seth Shulman, *Owning the Future*, Houghton Mifflin, Boston, 1999, p. 3.
22. Ibid., p. 1.
23. Ibid., pp. 5, 158.
24. Ibid., pp. 13, 173.
25. Ibid., p. 181.
26. *Los Angeles Times*, February 21, 1999.
27. *Business Week*, "Field of Genes," April 12, 1999.
28. Miguel Altieri, "The Ecological Impacts of Transgenic Crops on Agroecosystem Health," Department of Environmental Science, University of California, Berkeley.
29. Ibid.
30. "Field of Genes," *Business Week*, April 12, 1999.
31. Food First Action Alert, "Urgent Action Needed on Terminator Technology," February 12, 1999, Oakland, California.
32. Josephson, Robber Barons, p. 360.
33. Ben H. Bagdikian, *The Media Monopoly*, (fifth ed.) Beacon Press, Boston, 1997, p. ix.
34. Edward S. Herman and Robert W. McChesney, *The Global Media: The New Missionaries of Corporate Capitalism*, Cassell, London & Washington D.C., 1997 pp. 70–94.
35. Herman and McChesney, *Global Media*, p. 71.
36. Ibid., p. 37.
37. Bagdikian, *Media Monopoly*, p. xv.
38. Ibid., pp. xiv–xvi.
39. Josephson, *Robber Barons*, p. 407.
40. "Trillion Dollar Banks," *Business Week*, April 27, 1998.
41. "Fast-Forward for Finance," *Business Week*, August 31, 1998.
42. Susan Strange, *Mad Money: When Markets Outgrow Governments*, University of Michigan Press, Ann Arbor, 1998, p. 24.
43. "The 21st Century Economy," *Business Week*, August 31, 1998.
44. "A Tale of Two Economies," *Fortune*, April, 1999.
45. Strange, pp. 29–31.
46. Ibid., p. 123.
47. "The Citi That Slept," *Business Week*, November 2, 1998, pp. 94–100.
48. Josephson, *Robber Barons*, p. viii.
49. Ibid., p. 317.
50. "Candidates Falling into the Finally Open Arms of High Technology," *New York Times*, May 11, 1999.
51. "The High-Tech Lobby Is Learning Fast," *Business Week*, April 19, 1999
52. Ibid.

53. "Candidates Falling into the Finally Open Arms of High Technology," *New York Times*, May 11, 1999.
54. Todd Gitlin, *Conglomerates and the Media*, The New Press, New York, 1997, p. 12.

CHAPTER 4

1. See Francis Fukuyama, *The End of History and the Last Man*, The Free Press, New York, 1992.
2. See United Nations Development Program, *UNDP Report*, United Nations, New York, 1998.
3. Perry Anderson, *The Origins of Postmodernity*, Verso, London & New York, 1998, p. 62.
4. See Terry Nichols Clark and Michael Rempel, *Citizen Politics in Post-Industrial Societies*, Westview Press, Boulder, CO, 1997.
5. See Amy Kaplan and Donald Pease (eds), *Cultures of United States Imperialism*, Duke University Press, Durham, 1993.
6. Maria del Carmen Suescum Pozas, "From Reading to Seeing: Doing and Undoing Imperialism in the Visual Arts," in Gilbert M. Joseph, Catherine C. LeGrand, and Ricardo D. Salvatore (eds), *Close Encounters of Empire*, Duke University Press, Durham & London, 1998, pp. 525–56.
7. Honi Fern Haber, *Beyond Postmodern Politics: Lyotard, Rorty, Foucault*, Routledge, New York, 1994, p. 113.
8. Ibid., p. 124.
9. Ibid.
10. Glenn Jordan and Chris Weedon, *Cultural Politics: Class, Gender, Race and the Postmodern World*, Blackwell, Oxford, UK and Cambridge, MA, 1995, p. 545.
11. Ibid., p. 547.
12. Ibid., p. 564.
13. Hans-Georg Betz, *Postmodern Politics in Germany*, St Martin's Press, New York, 1991, p. 4.
14. Ibid., p. 10.
15. Ibid., p. 94.
16. Pat Buchanan, "Onward, Conservative Soldiers," in *San Francisco Examiner*, February 21, 1999.
17. Ariel Salleh, *Ecofeminism as Politics: Nature, Marx and the Postmodern*, Zed Books, New York, 1997, p. 192.
18. For an outstanding example of how the web can be used for a people to reclaim their history, see www.akaKURDISTAN.com. This site is a collection of pictorial and oral materials of the Kurdish community that had been dispersed throughout the world over the past century. The web site continues the work begun by Susan Meisalas in Kurdistan: *In the Shadow of History*, Random House, New York, 1997.
19. Coordinadora Civil Para La Emergencia y La Reconstruccion, "Covirtiendo la Tragedia del Mitch en Una Oportunidad para el Desarrollo humao y Sostenible de Nicaragua," Managua, Nicaragua, May, 1999.

CHAPTER 5

1. Russell Jacoby, *The End of Utopia: Politics and Culture in an Age of Apathy*, Basic Books, New York, p. 7.
2. Ellen Meiksins Wood is one of the major critics of attempts to find common ground between Marxism and postmodernism. See Ellen Meiksins Wood, "Modernity, Postmodernity, or Capitalism?" *Monthly Review*, 48, July–August, 1996, pp. 21–39.
3. The term "strong" postmodernism is borrowed from Barbara Epstein. She, however, does not link up the "soft" postmodernist position with Marxism, but argues generally that "postmodernism has become an obstacle to addressing urgent issues." See Barbara Epstein, "Postmodernism and the Left," *New Politics*, No. 6 Winter, 1997, pp. 130–44.
4. See Ernesto Laclau and Chantal Mouffe, *Hegemony and Socialist Strategy: Towards a Radical Democratic Politics*, Verso, London and New York, 1985. See also M. Barrett, *The Politics of Truth: From Marx to Foucault*, Stanford University Press, Stanford, CA, 1991.
5. Stephen Resnick and Richard Wolff, *Knowledge and Class: A Marxian Critique of Political Economy*, University of Chicago Press, Chicago, 1987.
6. For recent essays by Balibar and Negri as well as other articles relating to postmodern Marxism, see Antonio Callari and David F. Ruccio (eds), *Postmodern Materialism and the Future of Marxist Theory: Essays in the Althusserian Tradition*, Wesleyan University Press, Hanover and London, 1996.
7. J.K. Gibson-Graham, *The End of Capitalism (As We Knew It): A Feminist Critique of Political Economy*, Blackwell, London, 1996, p. 6.
8. Frederic Jameson, "Actually Existing Marxism," in S. Makdisi, C. Casarino and R.E. Karl (eds), *In Marxism Beyond Marxism*, Routledge, New York, 1996, p. 54.
9. See Edward W. Soja, *Postmodern Geographies: The Reassertion of Space in Critical Social Theory*, Verso, New York & London, 1989.
10. Stuart Hall, *The Hard Road to Renewal: Thatcherism and the Crisis of the Left*, Verso, London & New York, 1988. See also Stuart Hall and Paul du Gay (eds), *Questions of Cultural Identity*, Sage Publications, Thousand Oaks, CA, 1996.
11. Marshall Berman, *All That Is Solid Melts Into Air*, London, Verso, 1983.
12. Several key essays on postmodernism and Marxism published by *New Left Review* are: Jeffrey C. Alexander, "Modern, Anti, Post and Neo." *New Left Review*, No. 211, May–June, 1995 pp. 63–101; Goran Therborn, "Dialectics of Modernity: On Critical Theory and the Legacy of Twentieth-Century Marxism." *New Left Review*, No. 215 January–February, 1996, pp. 59–81; Gregor McLennan, "Post-Marxism and the 'Four Sins' of Modernist Theorizing," *New Left Review*, July–August 1996. Alexander's article argues that a new school of thought, "neo-modernism," may already be challenging postmodernism. McLennan's essay is an attempt to defend Marxism against more extreme and inaccurate postmodernist attacks, while at the same time recognizing that there have been reductionist and other tendencies of Marxism that postmodernists have criticized.

13. Michael Ryan, *Marxism and Deconstruction: A Critical Articulation*, The Johns Hopkins University Press, Baltimore, 1982, p. 1.
14. Meiksins Wood, "Modernity, Postmodernity or Capitalism," p. 27.
15. Ibid., p. 32.
16. Michael J. Watts and Allan Pred, *Reworking Modernity: Capitalisms and Symbolic Discontent*, Rutgers University Press, New Brunswick, NJ, 1992, p. 13.
17. David Spadafora, *The Idea of Progress in Eighteenth-Century Britain*, Yale University Press, New Haven & London, 1990, p. 381.
18. Meiksins Wood distorts my own critique of the Enlightenment in a previous article. She quotes me as saying that the "Enlightenment project" and "Enlightenment values" are "at the root of the disasters that have wracked humanity throughout this century." See Meiksins Wood, "Modernity, Postmodernity or Capitalism," p. 27. In fact I said that "what I find particularly useful in postmodernism at this ideological juncture is its view that there are no absolute laws of history as well as its contention that modernism and the faith in progress that began in the age of Enlightenment are at the root of the disasters ..." While "hard" postmodernists may reject the entire Enlightenment, this is not my position. See Roger Burbach, "For a Zapatista Style Postmodernist Perspective," *Monthly Review*, No. 47 March, p. 37.
19. Arturo Escobar, *Encountering Development: The Making and Unmaking of the Third World*, Princeton University Press, Princeton, 1995, p. 39.
20. Ibid., p. 4.
21. Ponna Wignaraja (ed.), *New Social Movements in the South: Empowering the People*, Zed Books, London & New Jersey, 1993, p.13.
22. The resurgence, or reactivation, of the U.S. labor movement with the election of John Sweeney as president of the AFL-CIO is certainly an important development that illustrates the critical importance of the labor movement in any process of social change. But it is important to note that the new activists of the AFL-CIO are reaching out to other sectors on the basis of gender and race and are building bridges to the social movements.
23. Fernando Calderon, Alejandro Piscitelli and J. L. Reyna, "Social Movements: Actors, Theories, Expectations," in A. Escobar and Sonia E. Alvarez (eds), *The Making of Social Movements in Latin America*, Westview Press, Boulder, CO, 1992, pp. 23–24.
24. See Doug Henwood, "Post What?" *Monthly Review*, 48, September 1996. See also Jeremey Rifkin, *The End of Work: The Decline of the Global Labor Force and the Dawn of the Post-Market Era*, GP Putnam's Sons, New York, 1995.

CHAPTER 6

1. See Kevin Danaher and Roger Burbach (eds), *Globalize This! The Battle Against the World Trade Organization and Corporate Rule*, Common Courage Press, Monroe, Maine, 2000.

2. J.K. Gibson-Graham, *The End of Capitalism (As We Knew It): A Feminist Critique of Political Economy*, Blackwell, London, 1996.
3. Geoffrey M. Hodgson in *Economics and Utopia, Why the Learning Economy is not the End of History*, Routledge, London & New York, 1999, pp. 205–15.
4. Ibid. pp. 189, 213.
5. *San Francisco Chronicle*, March 3, 2000.
6. Hodgson, *Economics and Utopia*, pp. 213–15.
7. Ibid., pp. 241–48.
8. David Korten, *The Post-Corporate World: Life After Capitalism*, Berrett-Koehler, San Francisco, and Kumarian Press, West Hartford, CT, 1999, p. 151.
9. Ibid., p. 178.
10. Michael Shuman, *Going Local: Creating Self-Reliant Communities in a Global Age*, Free Press, New York, 1998, pp. 28–29.
11. Brian K. Murphy, *Transforming Ourselves, Transforming the World: An Open Conspiracy for Social Change*, Zed Books, London, Inter Pares, Ottawa, Fernwood Publishing, Halifax, 1999, pp. 13–26.
12. Ibid., pp. 33–35.
13. Ibid., p. 81.
14. See Danaher and Burbach, *Globalize This!* This section draws on the introduction of that book.
15. William Greider, "AFL-CIO Goes Global," *The Nation*, March 20, 2000.

CHAPTER 7

1. Judith Adler Hellman, "Social Movements: Revolution, Reform and Reaction," NACLA *Report on the Americas*, Vol. 30, No. 6, May/June, 1997, pp. 13–18.
2. William I. Robinson, *Promoting Polyarchy: Globalization, U.S. Intervention and Hegemony*, Cambridge, Great Britain: Cambridge University Press, 1996.
3. For an extensive discussion of democracy and its relationship to neo-liberalism and the struggles of the left, see Steve Volk's anniversary essay "'Democracy' Versus 'Democracy'", NACLA *Report on the Americas*, Vol. 30, No. 4, Jan/Feb, 1997, pp. 6–12.
4. See especially one of NACLA's most important ground-breaking reports: Elizabeth Farnsworth, Richard Feinberg and Eric Leenson, "Facing the Blockade," January, 1973.
5. Jorge G. Castenada, *Utopia Unarmed: The Latin American Left After the Cold War*, Alfred A. Knopf, New York 1993, p. 432.
6. James Petras, "The Peasantry Strikes Back," *New Left Review*, No. 223, May/June, 1997, pp. 17–47.
7. See ISLA Special Report, *Ecuador, Reflections on the January, 2000 Popular Uprising*, by Guillermo Delgado-P., at <www.igc.org/isla/special>.
8. "Unity, Dignity, Autonomy: A Profile of CONAIE President Antonio Vargas," NACLA *Report*, March–April, 2000, p. 43.

9. For an extended discussion of alternative economies, see Roger Burbach, Orlando Nunez, and Boris Kagarlitsky, *Globalization And Its Discontents: The Rise of Postmodern Socialisms*, Pluto Press, London: 1997.
10. Ibid., *La Economia Popular*, pp. 289–312.
11. Roger Burbach, "Pinochet's Trial and Tribulations," Unpublished article, March 25, 2000. For copy email: censa@igc.org.
12. "Voices on the Left," NACLA *Report*, Vol. 30, No. 1, July/August, 1997, pp. 5–6.
13. Ibid., p. 5.

CHAPTER 8

1. The term "postmodern" is used broadly in this essay, similar to the way David Harvey employs it in *The Condition of Postmodernity*, Basil Blackwell Ltd., Cambridge, Massachusetts, 1989.
2. Based on interviews with EZLN representatives by Medea Benjamin of Global Exchange, San Francisco.
3. Agenda Estadistica de Chiapas, 1993, Secretaria de Programacion y Presupuesto, Direccion de Informatica, Geografia y Estadistica, Tuxtla Gutierrez, Chiapas, 1993.
4. Benito Salvatierra Izaba, et al., "Perfil Epidemiologico y Grados de Marginacion," Centro de Investigaciones Ecologicas del Sureste, San Cristobal de las Casas, March, 1994, pp. 3, 8.
5. Ibid., p. 10.
6. Robert Wasserstrom, *Class and Society in Central Chiapas*, University of California Press, Berkeley, 1983, pp. 112–19, 152.
7. Maria Eugenia Reyes Ramos, *El Reparto de Tierras y la Politica Agraria en Chiapas, 1914–1988*, Universidad Nacional Autonoma de Mexico, 1992, pp. 76–83.
8. See, for example, George A. Collier, *Fields of the Tzotzil: The Ecological Bases of Tradition in Highland Chiapas*, University of Texas Press, Austin, 1975, and Wasserstrom, *Class and Society*.
9. Jose Luis Pontigo Sanchez, "La Ganaderia Bovina en Dos Regiones de Chiapas: Costa y Norte," Centro de Investigaciones Ecologicas del Sureste, San Cristobal de las Casas, Enero, 1988, p. 14.
10. Daniel Villafuerte Solis, "La Economia Chiapaneca en los Ochenta," in *Anuario de Cultura e Investigacion 1990*, Instituto Chiapaneco de Cultura, Chiapas, 1990, pp. 176–78.
11. Pontigo Sanchez, "La Ganaderia Bovina ," pp. 2, 17.
12. Ibid., pp. 11, 12.
13. Universidad Autonoma de Chiapas, *Industria Petrolera y Desarollo Regional en Chiapas*, Tuxtla Gutierrez, 1988, pp. 16–23.
14. Roberto Thompson Gonzalez, *Explotacion Petrolera y Problematica Agraria en el Sureste de Mexico*, Centro de Investigaciones Ecologicas del Sureste, San Cristobal de las Casas, 1989, pp. 283–85.
15. Erwin Rodriguez, *Reforma Agraria: Cambio Estructural en Chiapas: Avances y Perspectives*, Universidad Autonoma de Chiapas, Tuxtla Gutierrez, 1988, p. 28.

16. Neil Harvey, "Power and Resistance in Contemporary Chiapas," Research Workshop on Power and Ethnicity in Guatemala and Chiapas, University of Texas at Austin, March 27–28, 1992, pp. 14–15.
17. Ibid., pp. 16–19.
18. Rodriguez, *Reforma Agraria*, p. 29.
19. Reyes Ramos, *El Reparto de Tierras*, pp. 118–19.
20. Rodriguez, *Reforma Agraria*, pp. 45–46.
21. Reyes Ramos, *El Reparto de Tierras*, p. 117.
22. Ibid., p. 119.
23. Neil Harvey, "Rebellion in Chiapas", in *Transformation of Rural Mexico*, No. 5, Center for U.S.-Mexican Studies, University of California at San Diego, 1994, pp. 9,12.
24. Ibid., and Daniel Villafuerte Solis, et al. "Problemas y Perspectivas del Desarrollo de la Ganaderia Bovina en Chiapas," Ponencia presentada a la Reunion Estatal de Ganaderia, Diciembre, 1991, Tuxtla Gutierrez, p. 4.
25. George A. Collier, *Seeking Food and Seeking Money: Changing Productive Relations in a Highland Mexican Community*, Discussion Paper 11, United Nations Research Institute for Social Development, May 1990, pp. 1–2.
26. Agenda Estadistica de Chiapas, 1993.
27. See Minnesota Advocates for Human Rights, *Civilians at Risk: Military and Police Abuses in Mexico's Countryside*, World Policy Institute, July, 1993.
28. Harvey, "Rebellion in Chiapas," p. 35.

CHAPTER 9

1. Marcos, cited in John Ross, *Rebellion from the Roots*, Common Courage, Maine, 1995, p. 153
2. Clandestine Revolutionary Indigenous Committee (CCRI) of the EZLN, reprinted in Lopez et al. (eds), *Shadows of Tender Fury: The Letters and Communiqués of Sub-commandante Marcos and the Zapatista Army of National Liberation*, Monthly Review Press, New York, 1995, p. 55.
3. Ibid, p. 72.
4. *Accion Zapatista*, "Cultural Aspects of Neoliberalism." From series on Zapatismo and various aspects of globalization and neo-liberalism, 1996.
5. CCRI of the EZLN, reprinted in John Holloway and Eloina Pelaez, "Introduction: Reinventing Revolution," in John Holloway and Eloina Pelaez (eds), *Zapatista! Reinventing Revolution in Mexico*, Pluto Press, London, 1998, p. 4.
6. Holloway and Pelaez, "Introduction," p. 17.
7. Patricia King and Francisco Javier Villanueva, "Breaking the Blockade: The Move from Jungle to City," in Holloway and Pelaez (eds), *Zapatista!*, p. 122.
8. Marcos, letter to civil society, August 30, 1996, distributed by Nuevo Amencer Press.
9. EZLN, communiqué, January 20, 1994. Reprinted in Lopez et al., *Shadows*, p. 86.

10. Harry Cleaver, "Computer-linked Social Movements and the Global Threat to Capitalism," published on the Internet at <http://www.eco.utexas.edu/faculty/Cleaver/polnet.html>.

11. EZLN communiqué May 28, 1994. Reprinted in *Zapatistas! Documents of the New Mexican Revolution,* Autonomedia, New York, 1995, pp. 310–11.

12. June Nash, "The Fiesta of the Word: The Zapatista Uprising and Radical Democracy in Mexico," *American Anthropologist* 99 (2) 1997, p. 261.

13. Marcos, communiqué date January 20, 1994. Reprinted in Lopez et al., *Shadows*, p. 85.

14. Holloway and Pelaez (eds), *Zapatista!*, p. 12.

15. CCRI of the EZLN, January 6, 1996.

16. The "Aguascalientes" are in the Zapatista territory and named in tribute to the Sovereign Revolutionary Convention that took place between October and November 1914 in the town of Aguascalientes which, according to Rajchenberg and Heau-Lambert, "had represented the most democratic moment in the course of the Mexican Revolution, and perhaps for that reason, the one which had been most overlooked by historians." See Holloway and Pelaez (eds), *Zapatista!*, p. 21. This was the name given to the space the Zapatistas carved out of the jungle to convene the first National Democratic Convention in June 1994 and expanded for the Intercontinental meeting.

17. Excerpt from the words of the EZLN in the closing act of the First Intercontinental Encounter for Humanity and Against Neo-Liberalism—read by Sub-commandante Marcos, August 1996.

18. Ibid.

19. Gustavo Lins-Ribiero, "Cybercultural Politics: Political Activism at a Distance in a Transnational World," in Sonia Alvarez et al. (eds), *Cultures of Politics, Politics of Cultures*, Westview Press, Boulder, 1998, p. 329.

20. Harry Cleaver, "The Zapatistas and the Electronic Fabric of Struggle," in Holloway and Pelaez (eds), *Zapatistas!*, pp. 81–103.

21. Ibid.

22. Lins-Ribiero, "Cybercultural Politics," p. 327.

23. *Accion Zapatista*, "Zapatismo in Cyberspace," 1996.

EPILOGUE

1. "They Say They Want A Revolution," *Business Week*, April 20, 2000.

2. *Washington Post*, April 16, 2000.

3. "They Say They Want A Revolution," *Business Week*.

4. Joseph Stiglitz, "What I Learned at the World Economic Crisis: The Insider," *The New Republic*, April 17, 2000.

5. *Washington Post*, April 16, 2000.

6. James D. Wolfensohn, Remarks at the Tenth Ministerial Meeting of UNCTAD, Rethinking Development—Challenges and Opportunities," Bangkok, Thailand, February 16, 2000.

7. "The IMF: Dr. Death? A Case Study of How the Global Banker's Shock Therapy Helps Economies but Hammers the Poor," *Time Magazine*, April 24, 2000.

Bibliography

Agenda Estadistica de Chiapas, Secretaria de Programacion y Presupuesto, Direccion de Informatica, Geografia y Estadistica, Tuxtla Gutierrez, Chiapas, 1993.

Akdogan, Haluk, *The Integration of International Capital Markets: Theory and Empirical Evidence*, Edward Elgar, Vermont, 1995.

Alexander, Jeffrey C., "Modern, Anti, Post and Neo," *New Left Review*, No. 211, May–June, 1995.

Altieri, Miguel, "The Ecological Impacts of Transgenic Crops on Agroecosystem Health," Department of Environmental Science, University of California, Berkeley.

Anderson, Perry, *The Origins of Postmodernity*, Verso, London & New York, 1998.

Arrighi, Giovanni, *The Long Twentieth Century: Money, Power, and the Origins of Our Times*, Verso, London, 1994.

Bacon, David, "The New Face of Union Busting," January 13, 1996, Email story. For copy email: dbacon@igc.org.

Bagdikian, Ben H., *The Media Monopoly*, 5th ed., Beacon Press, Boston, 1997.

Barrett, Michele, *The Politics of Truth: From Marx to Foucault*, Stanford University Press, Stanford, CA, 1991.

Benner, Chris, *Growing Together or Drifting Apart, A Status Report on Social and Economic Well-Being in Silicon Valley*, a joint publication of Working Partnerships USA and the Economic Policy Institute, January, 1998.

Berman, Marshall, *All That Is Solid Melts Into Air*, London, Verso, 1983.

Betz, Hans-Geor, *Postmodern Politics in Germany*, St Martin's Press, New York, 1991.

Buchanan, Pat, "Onward, Conservative Soldiers", in *San Francisco Examiner*, February 21, 1999.

Burbach, Roger, "The Conflict at Home and Abroad: U.S. Imperialism vs. the New Revolutionary Societies," in Richard Fagen, Carmen Diana Deere, and Jose Luis Coraggio (eds), *Monthly Review Press* New York, 1986.

——, "Roots of the Postmodern Rebellion in Chiapas," *New Left Review*, No. 205, May–June, 1994.

——, "For a Zapatista Style Postmodernist Perspective," *Monthly Review*, No. 47, March, 1996.

——, "Socialism is Dead, Long Live Socialism," NACLA *Report on the Americas*, November–December, 1997.

——, "The Rise of Postmodern Marxism: Or Virtually Existing Socialisms," URPE Newsletter, Winter, 4–5, 1997.

——, "The (Un)defining of Postmodern Marxism: On Narrating New Social and Economic Actors," *Rethinking Marxism*, Spring, 1998.

——, "Pinochet's Trial and Tribulations," Unpublished article, March 25, 2000. For a copy, email: censa@igc.org.

——, and William I. Robinson, "The Fin de Siecle Debate: Globalization as Epochal Shift," *Science and Society*, Spring, 1998.

——, Orlando Nunez, and Boris Kagarlitsky, *Globalization And Its Discontents: The Rise of Postmodern Socialisms*, Pluto Press, London & New York, 1997.

Burstein, Daniel and David Kline, *Road Warriors: Dreams and Nightmares Along the Information Highway*, Dutton Press, New York, 1995.

Business Week, "Trillion Dollar Banks," April 27, 1998.

——, "Psst! Want a Nice Pice of a Chaebol," May 18, 1998.

——, "Fast-Forward for Finance," August 31, 1998.

——, "The 21st Century Economy," August 31, 1998.

——, "The Citi That Slept," November 2, 1998.

——, "CBS: Can CEO Mel Karmazin Reinvent Network TV?," April 5, 1999.

——, "Fast, Cheap, and Ahead of the Pack," April 5, 1999.

——, "Field of Genes," April 12, 1999.

——, "Is Greed Good?," April 19, 1999.

——, "John Malone: Weaving a New Web," April 19, 1999.

——, "The High-Tech Lobby Is Learning Fast," April 19, 1999.

——, "They Say They Want A Revolution," April 20, 2000.

Calderon, Alvaro, Michael Mortimore and Wilson Peres, "Mexico: Foreign Investment as a Source of International Competitiveness," in John H. Dunning and Rafneesh Narula (eds), *Foreign Direct Investment and Governments*, Routledge, New York & London, 1996.

Calderon, Fernando, Alejandro Piscitelli and J. L. Reyna, "Social Movements: Actors, Theories, Expectations," in A. Escobar and Sonia E. Alvarez (eds), *The Making of Social Movements in Latin America*, Westview Press, Boulder, CO, 1992.

Callari, Antonio, and David F. Ruccio (eds), *Postmodern Materialism and the Future of Marxist Theory: Essays in the Althusserian Tradition*, Wesleyan University Press, Hanover and London, 1996.

Carmen Suescum Pozas, Maria del "From Reading to Seeing: Doing and Undoing Imperialism in the Visual Arts," in Gilbert M. Joseph, Catherine C. LeGrand, and Ricardo D. Salvatore (eds), *Close Encounters of Empire*, Duke University Press, Durham & London, 1998.

Castaneda, Jorge, *Utopia Unarmed*, Vintage, New York, 1993.

——, *Utopia Unarmed: The Latin American Left After the Cold War*, Alfred A. Knopf, New York, 1993.

Castells, Manuel, *The Information Age*, Vols 1–3, Blackwell Publishers, Cambridge, MA, 1996–1998.

——, *The Information Age*, Vol. 2, "The Power of Identity", Blackwell, Cambridge, MA, 1997.

Chossudovsky, Michel, *The Globalisation of Poverty: Impacts of IMF and World Bank Reforms*, Zed Books, London and NJ, Third World Network, Penang, Malaysia, 1997.

Clark, Terry Nichols and Michael Rempel, *Citizen Politics in Post-Industrial Societies*, Westview Press, Boulder, CO, 1997.

Cleaver, Harry, "Computer-linked Social Movements and the Global Threat to Capitalism," published on the web at <http://www.eco.utexas.edu/faculty/Cleaver/polnet.html>, 1999.

——, "The Zapatistas and the International Circulation of Struggles," published on the web at: <http://flag.blackened.net/revolt/mexico/comment/international_circ.html>.

Collier, George A., *Fields of the Tzotzil: The Ecological Bases of Tradition in Highland Chiapas*, University of Texas Press, Austin, 1975.

——, "Seeking Food and Seeking Money: Changing Productive Relations in a Highland Mexican Community", Discussion Paper 11, United Nations Research Institute for Social Development, May 1990.

Coordinadora Civil Para La Emergencia y La Reconstruccion, "Covirtiendo la Tragedia del Mitch en Una Oportunidad para el Desarrollo humao y Sostenible de Nicaragua," Managua, Nicaragua, May, 1999.

Danaher, Kevin and Roger Burbach (eds), *Globalize This! The Battle Against the World Trade Organization and Corporate Rule*, Common Courage Press, Monroe, Maine, 2000.

Debray, Regis, "A Guerrilla with a Difference," *Le Monde*, May 14, 1996.

Dicken, Peter, *Global Shift: The Internationalization of Economic Activity*, Guilford Press, New York, 1992.

Dornbusch, Rubi, "Mexico Learned Its Lesson. Now, Will East Asia?," *Business Week*, October 13, 1997.

Du Boff, Richard D., Edward S. Herman, William K. Tabb, Ellen Meiksins Wood, "Debate on Globalization," *Monthly Review*, 49(6), 1997.

Economic Policy Institute and the Center on Budget and Policy Priorities, "Pulling Apart," Washington D.C., January 2000.

Economist, The, "Latin America's Economic Reforms," October 19, 1991.

Economist, The, "One World?," October 18, 1997.

Eden, Lorraine, and Maureen Appel Molot, 1993, "Insiders and Outsiders: Defining 'Who Is Us' in the North American Automobile Industry," in *Transnational Corporations*, UNCTAD, United Nations, 2(3), 1993.

Epstein, Barbara, "Postmodernism and the Left," in *New Politics*, No. 6, Winter, 1997.

Escobar, Arturo, *Encountering Development: The Making and Unmaking of the Third World*, Princeton University Press, Princeton, 1995.

EZLN communiqué, May 28, 1994. Reprinted in *Zapatistas! Documents of the New Mexican Revolution*, Autonomedia, New York, 1995.

Farnsworth, Elizabeth, Richard Feinberg and Eric Leenson, "Facing the Blockade," NACLA *Report on the Americas*, January, 1973.

Fern Haber, Honi, *Beyond Postmodern Politics: Lyotard, Rorty, Foucault*, Routledge, New York, 1994.

Food First Action Alert, "Urgent Action Needed on Terminator Technology," Oakland, California, February 12, 1999.

Fortune, "Bill Gates, Richest American Ever," August 4, 1997.

——, "A Tale of Two Economies," April 26, 1999.

Fukuyama, Francis, *The End of History and the Last Man*, The Free Press, New York, 1992.

Gibson-Graham, J.K., *The End of Capitalism (As We Knew It): A Feminist Critique of Political Economy*, Blackwell, London, 1996.

Gidgit Digit, "The Debate on the Tactic of Electronic Civil Disobedience," posted on the Chiapas 1995 electronic network, August 15, 1998.

Gitlin, Todd, *Conglomerates and the Media*, The New Press, New York, 1997.

Gonzalez, Roberto Thompson, *Explotacion Petrolera y Problematica Agraria en el Sureste de Mexico*, Centro de Investigaciones Ecologicas del Sureste, San Cristobal de las Casas, 1989.

Gray, John, *False Dawn: The Delusions of Global Capitalism*, The New Press, New York, 1998.

Greider, William "Global Agenda: After the WTO Protest in Seattle, It's Time to Go on the Offensive. Here's How," *The Nation*, January 31, 2000.

——, "AFL-CIO Goes Global," *The Nation*, March 20, 2000.

Hall, Stuart, *The Hard Road to Renewal: Thatcherism and the Crisis of the Left*, Verso, London & New York, 1988.

Hall, Stuart and Paul du Gay (eds), *Questions of Cultural Identity*, Sage Publications, Thousand Oaks, CA, 1996.

Harvey, David, *Condition of Postmodernity*, Basil Blackwell Ltd., Cambridge, Massachusetts, 1989.

Harvey, Neil, "Power and Resistance in Contemporary Chiapas," paper presented at research workshop on power and ethnicity in Guatemala and Chiapas, University of Texas at Austin, March 27–28, 1992.

——, "Rebellion in Chiapas," in *Transformation of Rural Mexico*, No. 5, Center for U.S.-Mexican Studies, University of California at San Diego, 1994.

Hellman, Judith Adler, "Social Movements: Revolution, Reform and Reaction," NACLA *Report on the Americas*, May–June, 1997.

Henwood, Doug, "Post What?" *Monthly Review*, 48 (September) 1996.

Herman, Edward S., and Robert W. McChesney, *The Global Media: The New Missionaries of Corporate Capitalism*, Cassell, London & Washington, D.C., 1997.

Hilferding, Rudolf, *Finance Capital: A Study of the Latest Phase of Capitalist Development*, Routledge, Boston & London, 1981.

Hobsbawm, Eric, *The Age of Revolution*, Mentor, New York, 1962.

——, *The Age of Capital*, Sphere, London, 1977.

——, *The Age of Empire*, Pantheon, New York, 1987.

——, *The Age of Extremes*, Vintage, New York, 1994.

Hodgson, Geoffrey M. *Economics and Utopia, Why the Learning Economy is Not the End of History*, Routledge, London & New York, 1999.

Holloway, John, and Eloina Pelaez (eds), *Zapatista! Reinventing Revolution in Mexico*, Pluto Press, London, 1998.

International Labor Organization (ILO), *World Employment Report 1996–97*, United Nations, Geneva, 1997.

ISLA Special Report, "Ecuador, Reflections on the January, 2000 Popular Uprising," by Guillermo Delgado-P., at <www.igc.org/isla/special>.

Jacoby, Russell, *The End of Utopia: Politics and Culture in an Age of Apathy*, Basic Books, New York, 1999.

Jameson, Frederic, "Actually Existing Marxism," in S. Makdisi, C. Casarino and R.E. Karl (eds), *Marxism Beyond Marxism*, Routledge, New York, 1996.

Jordan Glenn, and Chris Weedon, *Cultural Politics: Class, Gender, Race and the Postmodern World*, Blackwell, Oxford, UK and Cambridge, MA, 1995.

Josephson, Matthew, *The Robber Barons: The Great American Capitalists*, 1861–1901, Harcourt, Brace & Co., New York, 1934, p. vii.

Kaplan, Amy and Donald Pease (eds), *Cultures of United States Imperialism*, Duke University Press, Durham, 1993.

Katz, Frederich, Interview, "La Revolucion Mexicana ... Una Revolucion que Sobrevive," Sociedad y Estado, Universidad de Guadalajara, Enero–Abril, 1992.

Korten, David, *The Post-Corporate World: Life After Capitalism*, Berrett-Koehler, San Francisco, and Kumarian Press, West Hartford, CT, 1999.

Krebs, Al, "The Calamity Howler," *The Progressive Populist*, January 1–15, 2000.

Laclau, Ernesto and Chantal Mouffe, *Hegemony and Socialist Strategy: Towards a Radical Democratic Politics*, Verso, London and New York, 1985.

Lins Ribiero, Gustavo, "Cybercultural Politics: Political Activism at a Distance in a Transnational World," in Sonia Alvarez et al. (eds), *Cultures of Politics, Politics of Cultures*, Westview Press, Boulder, 1998.

Marcos, letter to civil society August 30, 1996, distributed by Nuevo Amencer Press.

Marcos, Subcomandante., Shadows of Tender Fury: The Letters and Communiqués of Subcomandante Marcos and the Zapatista Army of National Liberation, *Monthly Review Press*, New York, 1995.

Marichal, Carlos, "Latin America in the Age of the Billionaires," NACLA *Report on the Americas*, May–June, 1997.

Martin, Hans-Peter and Harald Schumann, *The Global Trap: Globalization and the Assault on Prosperity and Democracy*, Zed Books, London & New York, 1997.

Mattera, Philip, *World Class Business: A Guide to the 100 Most Powerful Global Corporations*, Henry Holt, New York, 1992.

McLennan, Gregor, "Post-Marxism and the 'Four Sins' of Modernist Theorizing," *New Left Review*, July–August, 1996.

Meisalas, Susan, *Kurdistan: In the Shadow of History*, Random House, New York, 1997.

Minnesota Advocates for Human Rights, *Civilians at Risk: Military and Police Abuses in Mexico's Countryside*, World Policy Institute, July, 1993.

Murphy, Brian K., *Transforming Ourselves, Transforming the World: An Open Conspiracy for Social Change*, Zed Books, London, Inter Pares, Ottawa, Fernwood Publishing, Halifax, 1999.

NACLA *Report on the Americas*, "Voices on the Left," July–August, 1997.

Nash, June, "The Fiesta of the Word: The Zapatista Uprising and Radical Democracy in Mexico," *American Anthropologist* 99 (2) 1997.

Nunez, Orlando, *La Economia Popular: Asociativa y Autogestionaria*, CIPRES, Managua, 1995.

Petras, James, "The Peasantry Strikes Back," *New Left Review*, No. 223, May–June, 1997.

Pontigo Sanchez, Jose Luis, "La Ganaderia Bovina en Dos Regiones de Chiapas: Costa y Norte," Centro de Investigaciones Ecologicas del Sureste, San Cristobal de las Casas, Enero, 1988.

Reich, Robert, on National Public Radio, January 20, 2000.

Resnick, Stephen and Richard Wolff, *Knowledge and Class: A Marxian Critique of Political Economy*, University of Chicago Press, Chicago, 1987.

Reyes Ramos, Maria Eugenia, *El Reparto de Tierras y la Politica Agraria en Chiapas, 1914–1988*, Universidad Nacional Autonoma de Mexico, 1992.

Rifkin, Jeremey, *The End of Work: The Decline of the Global Labor Force and the Dawn of the Post-Market Era*, GP Putnam's Sons, New York, 1995.

Robinson, William I., *Promoting Polyarchy: Globalization, U.S. Intervention, and Hegemony*, Cambridge University Press, Cambridge, 1996.

Robinson, William I. "Globalisation: Nine Theses of Our Epoch," *Race and Class*, 38(2), 1996. Robinson, William I. "Maldevelopment in Central America: Globalization and Social Change," *Development and Change* 29(3) 1998.

Rodriguez, Erwin, *Reforma Agraria: Cambio Estructural en Chiapas: Avances y Perspectives*, Universidad Autonoma de Chiapas, Tuxtla Gutierrez, 1988.

Ross, John, *Rebellion from the Roots*, Common Courage, Maine. 1995.

Ryan, Michael, *Marxism and Deconstruction: A Critical Articulation*, The Johns Hopkins University Press, Baltimore, 1982.

Salleh, Ariel, *Ecofeminism as Politics: Nature, Marx and the Postmodern*, Zed Books, New York, 1997.

Salvatierra Izaba, Benito. et al., "Perfil Epidemiologico y Grados de Marginacion," Centro de Investigaciones Ecologicas del Sureste, San Cristobal de las Casas, March, 1994.

Sassoon, Donald, *One Hundred Years of Socialism: The West European Left in the Twentieth Century*, The New Press, New York, 1996.

Shulman, Seth, *Owning the Future*, Houghton Mifflin, Boston, 1999.

Shuman, Michael, *Going Local: Creating Self-Reliant Communities in a Global Age*, Free Press, New York, 1998.

Siegel, Lenny (ed.), *Global Electronics*, No. 124, Pacific Studies Center, Mountain View, CA, February 1994.

Sivanandan, A., and Ellen Meiksins Wood, "Globalization and Epochal Shifts: An Exchange," *Monthly Review*, 48(9): 1997.

Sklair, Leslie, *Sociology of the Global System*, (second revised edition), Johns Hopkins, Baltimore, 1995.

Soja, Edward W., *Postmodern Geographies: The Reassertion of Space in Critical Social Theory*, Verso, New York & London, 1989.

Spadafora, David, *The Idea of Progress in Eighteenth-Century Britain*, Yale University Press, New Haven & London, 1990.

Stiglitz, Joseph, "What I Learned at the World Economic Crisis: The Insider," *The New Republic*, April 17, 2000.

Strange, Susan, *Mad Money: When Markets Outgrow Governments*, University of Michigan Press, Ann Arbor, 1998.

Sweezy, Paul, "More (or Less) on Globalization," *Monthly Review*, 49(4) 1997.

Therborn, Goran, "Dialectics of Modernity: On Critical Theory and the Legacy of Twentieth-Century Marxism," *New Left Review*, No. 215, January–February, 1996.

Time, "The IMF: Dr. Death? A Case Study of How the Global Banker's Shock Therapy Helps Economies but Hammers the Poor," April 24, 2000.

Toffler, Alvin, *Powershift: Knowledge, Wealth, and Violence at the Edge of the 21st Century*, Bantam Books, New York, 1991.

UNCTAD, *1996 World Investment Report: Investment, Trade and International Policy Arrangements*, New York and Geneva: United Nations. 1996.

——, *1997 World Investment Report: Transnational Corporations, Market Structure and Competition Policy*, New York and Geneva: United Nations, 1997.

United Nations, Department of Economic and Social Information and Policy Analysis, *World Economic and Social Survey 1997*, United Nations, 1997.

United Nations Development Program, *UNDP Report, 1998*, UN Publications, New York, 1998.

——, *UNDP Report, 1999*, Overview, UN Publications, New York, 1999.

——, *United Nations Human Development Report, 1998*, United Nations, New York, 1998.

Universidad Autonoma de Chiapas, *Industria Petrolera y Desarollo Regional en Chiapas*, Tuxtla Gutierrez, 1988.

Vargas, Antonio, "Unity, Dignity, Autonomy: A Profile of CONAIE President Antonio Vargas," NACLA *Report on the Americas*, March–April, 2000.

Vidal, John, "Anatomy of a Nineties Revolution," *Guardian*, London, January 13, 1999.

Villafuerte Solis, Daniel "La Economia Chiapaneca en los Ochenta," in *Anuario de Cultura e Investigacion 1990*, Instituto Chiapaneco de Cultura, Chiapas, 1990.

Villafuerte Solis, Daniel, et al. "Problemas y Perspectivas del Desarrollo de la Ganaderia Bovina en Chiapas," Ponencia presentada a la Reunion Estatal de Ganaderia, Diciembre, 1991, Tuxtla Gutierrez.

Volk, Steve, "'Democracy' Versus 'Democracy'", NACLA *Report on the Americas*, No. 4, January–February, 1997.

Wasserstrom, Robert, *Class and Society in Central Chiapas*, University of California Press, Berkeley, 1983.

Waterman, Peter, *Globalisation, Social Movements and the New Internationalisms*, Cassell, London, 1998.

Watts, Michael J. and Allan Pred, *Reworking Modernity: Capitalisms and Symbolic Discontent*, Rutgers University Press, New Brunswick, NJ, 1992.

Weiss, Linda, "Globalization and the Myth of the Powerless State," *New Left Review*, September–October, 1997.

Weiss, Linda, *The Myth of the Powerless State*, Cornell University Press, Ithaca, New York, 1998.

Wignaraja, Ponna (ed.), *New Social Movements in the South: Empowering the People*, Zed Books, London & New Jersey, 1993.

Wolfensohn, James D., remarks at the tenth ministerial meeting of UNCTAD, "Rethinking Development—Challenges and Opportunities," Bangkok, Thailand, February 16, 2000.

Wood, Ellen Meiksins "Modernity, Postmodernity, or Capitalism?" *Monthly Review*, 48, July–August, 1996.

World Bank, *Global Economic Prospects and the Developing Countries*, World Bank, Washington, D.C., 1992.

Index

Compiled by Auriol Griffith-Jones